Stories of God's Love

Ages 3 and 4

Preschool Program

ONE-DAY GUIDE

Authors
Shauna M. Adams, EdD
Joy L. Comingore, MA
Joni L. Baldwin, EdD

Contributing Writers
Elizabeth M. Engelhardt, MA
Susan M. Ferguson, MS
Debra Ciambro Grisso, MEd

Advisors
Reverend Louis J. Cameli, STD
Judith Deckers, MEd
Mary Ann Dudko, PhD
Elaine McCarron, SCN, MDiv
Reverend Robert D. Duggan, STD
Marie K. Rein, SSJ, MEd

RCL
Benziger

Allen, Texas

"The Ad Hoc Committee to Oversee the Use of the Catechism, United States Conference of Catholic Bishops, has found the doctrinal content of this manual, copyright 2009, to be in conformity with the *Catechism of the Catholic Church.*"

RCL Benziger
DEVELOPMENT TEAM

Steven Ellair
James Spurgin
EDITORS

Lisa Brent
Tricia Legault
DESIGN

Jo Rotunno
DIRECTOR OF CREATIVE DEVELOPMENT

Kate Sweeney Ristow
NATIONAL CATECHETICAL CONSULTANT

Susan Smith
PHOTO RESEARCH

Laura Fremder
Jenna Nelson
PRODUCTION

Joseph Crisalli
Marybeth Jambor
AC Ware
WEB SITE

Ed DeStefano
EXECUTIVE DIRECTOR, EDITORIAL

Maryann Nead
PRESIDENT

Nihil Obstat
Rev. Msgr. Robert Coerver
Censor Librorum

Imprimatur
† Most Reverend Kevin J. Farrell, DD, Bishop of Dallas

November 5, 2007

The Nihil Obstat and Imprimatur are official declarations that the material reviewed is free of doctrinal or moral error. No implication is contained therein that those granting the Nihil Obstat and Imprimatur agree with the contents, opinions, or statements expressed.

ACKNOWLEDGMENTS

Excerpts from the *New American Bible* with Revised New Testament and Psalms Copyright © 1991, 1986, 1970 Confraternity of Christian Doctrine, Inc., Washington, DC. Used with permission. All rights reserved. No portion of the *New American Bible* may be reprinted without permission in writing from the copyright holder.

Excerpt from Preface for Thanksgiving Day © 1985 United States Conference of Catholic Bishops, Washington, DC. Used with permission. All rights reserved.

PHOTO CREDITS

Page 6, Chris Cheadle/Getty Images; 7, Ross Whitaker/Getty Images; 8, Jose Luis Pelaez/Getty Images; 9, RCLB; 10 (top), Inti St Clair/Getty Images; 10 (center), Sean Justice/Punchstock; 10 (bottom), iStockphoto; 11 (top), Altrendo Images/Getty Images; 11 (center), Nicole S. Young/iStockphoto; 11 (bottom), Gregory Costanzo/Getty Images; 24, Ariel Skelley/Getty Images; 25 (top), Monika Adamczyk/iStockphoto; 25 (bottom), BananaStock/Punchstock; 26, Corbis; 27, Realistic Reflections/Getty Images

Send all inquiries to:

RCL Benziger
206 East Bethany Drive
Allen, TX 75002-3804

Toll Free 877-275-4725
Fax   800-688-8356

Visit us at   www.RCLBenziger.com
              www.RCLBenzigerPreschool.com

Printed in the United States of America

20632 ISBN: 978-0-7829-1183-1 (One-Day Guide)

20631 ISBN: 978-0-7829-1182-4 (Children's Folder with Leaflets Set)
20633 ISBN: 978-0-7829-1184-8 (Multi-Day Guide)
20634 ISBN: 978-0-7829-1185-5 (Teaching Posters Set)
20640 ISBN: 978-0-7829-1190-9 (Songbook with CD)
20641 ISBN: 978-0-7829-1191-6 (Program Director's Manual)

2 3 4 5 6 7 8 • 14 13 12 11 10 09

Stories of God's Love Writing Team

Shauna Adams, EdD, is an Associate Professor of Early Childhood at the University of Dayton. She teaches graduate and undergraduate courses in child development, preschool curriculum and assessment, early childhood special education, and early childhood leadership and advocacy. As a product of Catholic schools, she enjoys working with Catholic School teachers as a consultant and campus liaison. Prior to teaching in higher education, Shauna taught students with special needs for 10 years. She earned a masters degree in counseling and a school psychology certificate and worked as a school psychologist. After having children of her own, Shauna became captivated with young children and earned her doctorate in Early Childhood and Special Education from the University of Cincinnati.

Joni Baldwin, EdD, is an Assistant Professor of Early Childhood at the University of Dayton. She teaches graduate and undergraduate courses in health and medical issues, assessment, and inclusion of the child with special needs. Dr. Baldwin has a long history of working with young children age birth to eight in Connecticut, Minnesota and Ohio. She has been a classroom teacher, an educational consultant to public schools, and a director of an early intervention program prior to teaching in higher education.

Joy L. Comingore, MA, earned her masters of arts with an emphasis in Christian education of young children and is currently employed in the Department of Teacher Education at the University of Dayton. Joy relies on her 15 years of experience in a pre-kindergarten classroom where she taught 3 to 6 year olds. Currently, she shares her experience in the preschool classroom with early childhood teacher education students as she supervises them in pre-kindergarten classroom practicum experiences. Joy presents at regional, state and national conferences and provides professional development for early childhood teachers. Providing quality education and religious training for young children is a professional and personal goal.

Beth Engelhardt, MA, is a fulltime clinical faculty member at the University of Dayton. She has over 30 years of experience in early childhood education, including 15 years as an administrator of an accredited Catholic child care center. She has also been an instructor at five area colleges, a child care licensing specialist, and serves as an advisor/mentor for Child Development Associate Certificate (CDA) students, student teachers and child care center directors. Beth authored *The Director Mentoring Program* and co-authored *Dayton's Children: A Resource Guide for Families.* Beth presents at local, state, and national conferences and is past president of the Dayton Association for Young Children. She is a member of the Montgomery County Early Childhood Coalition, and moderator for the Montgomery County Child Care Directors Online Group. Beth earned her master's degree in Leadership in Education and Human Development, Early Childhood Education, and Adult Education from Pacific Oaks College in Pasadena, California.

Susan Ferguson, MS, is the Director of the Center for Catholic Education at the University of Dayton. The Center mentors and places teachers in urban Catholic schools, offers support services to Catholic schools and collaborates with archdiocese and other University of Dayton departments to offer professional development opportunities to teachers. Susan also instructs undergraduate courses that introduce the profession of teaching to first year teacher education candidates and teaches other courses regarding child and adolescent development. Recently, she was asked to enter the Marianist Educational Associate program at the University of Dayton.

Debra Ciambro Grisso, MEd, has been a School Counselor for a public school in the Dayton, Ohio area for the past six years. As a counselor she deals with individual counseling issues, small support groups, and character education classes. Prior to earning her school counseling license from the University of Dayton, Debra taught Language Arts in the public schools for 21 years. Her master's degree is in Reading from the University of Louisville. Debra was selected to participate in the Writer's Workshop at Wright State University and has been published in the field of children's writing.

Contents

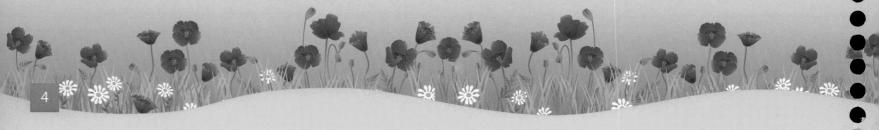

Unit Four • I Belong to My Church Family

Unit Five • I Tell God I Love Him

Unit Six • I Celebrate Holy Days and Holidays

Welcome to Stories of God's Love!

This year you will be a teacher in a religion readiness program that helps young children take their first steps on their journey of faith. *Stories of God's Love:*

- teaches children appropriate Scripture stories that tell them of God's love and connects these stories to the children's lives.
- follows the guidelines of the Catechism Committee of the United States Conference of Catholic Bishops to assist the review of preschool materials.
- incorporates a simple "Teach and Apply" process in every session.
- weaves prayer experiences into every lesson.
- connects your sessions to the home by offering weekly family enrichment.
- supports your religion coordinator with resources to make your religion readiness program effective and enjoyable.

Your Role

Beginning to teach from your new program can be a wonderful experience. As *Stories of God's Love* was being developed, you were thought about every step of the way. We considered the needs of both beginning teachers and the needs of experienced, veteran preschool educators. The result is teacher guides that will make a difference!

We created two guides for *Stories of God's Love:* a guide for those who teach one session per week, and one for those who offer religion sessions on multiple days. You'll find that the session plans are very simple and easy to use. They were written by people who actually teach religion readiness classes just like yours, so we know that these lessons will work for you.

This teacher guide has excellent organizational pages and background information on the topics that you will be teaching—hundreds of ideas you can use. Colorful Teaching Posters and a Music Songbook with CD are also available. In addition, we hope you'll become a regular visitor to our supportive Web site designed to offer even more ideas. You'll find it at **RCLBenzigerPreschool.com**.

We're looking forward to working with you!

The Catechetical Ministry

Preschool catechists and teachers do more than simply teach religion to their young learners. First of all, catechists are people of faith themselves who let the word of God echo, or resound, through their lives and teaching. Religion teachers and catechists share their faith and help the children to apply and live out their faith day by day.

If you are like most catechists and teachers, you may already have realized that teaching religion is different from most other teaching tasks. Certainly, your storytelling ability and skills for organizing cooperative play activities will serve you well. But there is a different atmosphere in faith formation because you are sharing your own faith as well as your knowledge.

You may be wondering what you are getting yourself into and asking how you can ever help children to grow in faith. You might also be wondering if you are up to the challenge. Well, you are! You are one of the thousands of catechists and teachers who have asked these same questions and have discovered a wonderful secret: Helping young children begin their journey of faith is one of the most important ministries of the Church and one of its most rewarding.

Here is a simple approach to your ministry that will make this year a satisfying one for you:

Relax! Some teachers and catechists find the idea of sharing faith a little frightening. Remember, the Scriptures tell us that our ancestors in faith, including Moses, Jeremiah, Peter, and Mary, faced the same fear. With God's help, they did great things. You will too.

Ask questions! You are not expected to have the answers to every question the children may ask. Your pastor, priests, principal, DRE, preschool coordinator, and other catechists will gladly help you respond to the children. We will too.

Take your time! Remember, you are both a teacher and a learner. Be patient with yourself as you learn. Trust in the Holy Spirit. The important thing is to continue to grow in your ministry.

Use your guide! In the pages that follow you'll find a comprehensive introduction to *Stories of God's Love,* including an overview of the effective and easy-to-use "teach and apply" format. You'll find hundreds of helpful tips and activities to engage young children in the lesson plans that follow. Gradually, you'll find yourself growing in competence and confidence about your ministry.

Examine the children's leaflets. Browsing through the children's leaflets, including the family pages, will help you to capture the flavor of what you are to present to the children. Becoming familiar with the sequence of lessons will also help you plan your calendar.

You are embarking on an exciting journey this year. Be sure to take advantage of all the opportunities for growth as a teacher that are offered by your parish or school. And most of all, have fun!

Getting Started

Your Children

Your success as a teacher depends on your relationship with the children. Welcome the children with warmth and enthusiasm. Be sure to tell them how much you look forward to getting to know them.

Here are some basic principles to keep in mind with all young people:

- Respect them as children of God.
- Honor the children's abilities, their imagination, and their desire to know and love God.
- Value the children as learners.
- Involve the children actively in the learning process.
- Help the children understand what a difference faith can make in their lives.

You will learn more about the special characteristics of three-, four- and five-year-old children on pages 10 and 11 of this guide.

Your Teaching Space

Every teacher and catechist faces the challenge of creating an inviting and safe catechetical teaching environment. With a little creativity and determination, you can transform your setting into a warm and inviting environment for the teaching of religion.

Here are some questions to discuss with your principal, DRE, or religion coordinator:

- What are the safe environment guidelines of your parish or diocese?
- Is your teaching space shared with others? Can you meet with the other people who use the space to discuss needs and to build a spirit of cooperation?
- Are the chairs, desks and tables the appropriate size for the children? Can the seating be rearranged for different activities?
- Can the lighting and temperature be adjusted for comfort?
- Is a chalkboard, a dry-erase board, or newsprint available?
- Are you allowed to tape posters or other materials to walls or bulletin boards?
- How will the children clean up after the activities?
- What electronic media equipment is available? How can you be trained to use that equipment?

Your Prayer Center

The prayer center is the heart of your catechetical teaching space. It tells the children that sharing faith together is a sacred activity. Gather with the children in or around the prayer center for prayer each time you meet with them.

Here are some practical ideas for creating a prayer center:

- Cover a small table with a cloth, preferably with a cloth that is the color of the current liturgical season or the liturgical feast you are celebrating.
- Place a crucifix on the wall or on the table in the prayer center.
- Place a candle on the table as a sign that Christ is the Light of the World. (Be sure to check and follow all fire regulations.)
- Enthrone an open Bible on the table by displaying pages from important passages for the day.
- Place a plant or other objects that symbolize the lesson theme in the prayer center. Invite the children to take turns helping you decorate the prayer center by bringing in objects from home that might be appropriate to symbolize the themes you are covering in class.

Your General Supplies

No matter how well equipped with materials your school and parish programs are, there will usually be additional materials that you will need. Here are some items to have on hand:

- Art supplies such as art paper, construction paper, poster board, newsprint, colored markers, crayons, glue, washable paints, paint brushes, paint smocks, appropriate safety scissors, tape and yarn.
- Audiovisuals such as DVDs and videos, photos, posters, and music tapes or CDs. *Stories of God's Love* Music CD and Songbook are available and specifically designed for this program.
- Materials for your prayer center such as a cloth, a Bible, a crucifix, a candle, a plant, and symbols for the liturgical seasons and feasts.
- A bulletin board reserved for displaying religious projects and education topics such as the liturgical seasons and feasts of the Church.

Who is the Preschool Child?

The development of three-, four- and five-year-olds varies greatly from child to child. Children in these age groups tend to enjoy the same active learning techniques. However, as you read these developmental descriptions, consider that three-year-olds may be at an entry level while five-year-olds are more likely to be working on mastery. Remember that typical preschoolers vary greatly in their development.

Physical Development

While older children may take physical development for granted, young children are generally very proud of their physical accomplishments. Whether growing taller, learning to catch a ball or climbing the ladder of a slide, these physical feats mean a lot to three-, four- and five-year-olds. Activities that capitalize on the preschooler's interest in and need for movement are necessary for instruction to be effective for this age group. In order to do this, be sure to expect your preschoolers:

- To be developing body awareness including the parts of their body and the ability to navigate their body gracefully through space.
- To be unaware of safety issues related to physical activity.
- To be developing both large muscle and small muscle (eye-hand) coordination.
- To enjoy moving their body to music.
- To enjoy some small motor skills, such as scribbling, pretend writing, cutting and gluing, coloring and painting. These skills are just emerging so reward the children's efforts and not the product.

Cognitive Development and Learning Skills

Young three-, four- and five-year-olds make great strides in cognitive development which refers to their growing ability to make meaning of the world around them. They start with what they know and they learn new concepts by comparing new concepts to those with which they are familiar. During these early years, children enjoy opportunities that develop their ability to reason, acquire new knowledge and to solve problems. You can expect your preschoolers:

- To be interested in nature but have gaps in their understanding of the world around them, especially the physical laws of nature.
- To use both fact and fantasy to make sense of their world and, at times, not be able to distinguish between truth and fiction.
- To look at the world through their eyes alone and have limited ability to understand the perspectives of others.
- To learn by touching and manipulating objects.
- To learn by talking to others and by asking a lot of questions.

Language Development

Preschoolers develop language at a rate that is astonishing to most adults. They are learning to share their thoughts, feelings and ideas through language, gestures and facial expressions. Language development is important to both cognitive development and to social and emotional development. If language and communication skills are underdeveloped, young children will likely struggle to understand the language of others or to express their own ideas and feelings. As you support your preschoolers' language development, you can expect them:

- To be learning the rules of language as well as the meaning of words.
- To practice new words, concepts and voice tones in pretend play.
- To copy adults as they imitate their words and expressions.
- To talk in short sentences.
- To understand one-step and some two-step directions.
- To listen to an interesting story for eight to ten minutes.

Social and Emotional Development

Social development refers to the preschoolers' ability to get along with others while emotional development speaks to their ability to develop a concept of "self." This self-concept is the child's mental image of their characteristics and capabilities. The child's understanding of "self" is important in their learning how to interact with others. The feelings that children develop about themselves and about the people around them lay the foundation for their ability to take the risk to make mistakes or learn new things. This "self-concept" is newly forming and is fragile. To help children develop both a positive view of themselves and of others, it is important to know that preschoolers are likely:

- To need to have their feelings and the feelings of others labeled and explained.
- To need positive support from others in order to learn to resolve conflicts.
- To be just developing the language of interaction.

Spiritual Growth and Development

As young children grow and develop spiritually, it is important to remember the cognitive limitations that exist in young children. This series is designed to help children lay a positive foundation for faith formation. The concepts are presented in a positive way that allows children to explore new ideas in safe and familiar terms. Maintaining a positive and responsive classroom will allow young children to explore the concepts while growing stronger in their relationship with God and the Church community.

Scope and Sequence

Ages Three and Four

UNIT FOUR

I Belong to My Church Family

UNIT FOUR FOCUS

We are friends of Jesus. The friends of Jesus are called the Church.

Chapter 15   Friends of Jesus

Major Concept: Jesus invites four fishermen to be his special friends.

Key Word: friends of Jesus

Bible Story: "Come, Follow Me"
Based on Matthew 4:18–22

Chapter 16   I Am a Friend of Jesus

Major Concept: I am a friend of Jesus. I like going to church.

Key Word: church (as building, the place Jesus' friends come together.)

Story: "The Remember Game"

Chapter 17   Jesus Has Many Friends

Major Concept: Jesus' friends invite others to become friends of Jesus.

Key Word: Apostles, invitation

Bible Story: "Jesus Makes Two New Friends"
Based on John 1:43–49

Chapter 18   My Church Friends

Major Concept: I join with other friends of Jesus at church.

Key Word: Church (the people, the community of Jesus' friends)

Story: "Carlos' Church Friends"

UNIT FIVE

I Tell God I Love Him

UNIT FIVE FOCUS

I talk to God and speak to him. I pray every day.

Chapter 19   David Talked with God

Major Concept: God chose David the shepherd boy to be his special friend. David talked and listened to God.

Key Word: pray

Bible Story: "God's Good Friend David"
Based on 1 Samuel 16:11-12, 18; Psalm 5:3; Psalm 17:6

Chapter 20   I Pray Every Day

Major Concept: I talk with God every day.

Key Word: prayer

Story: "Abby Says 'Thank You' to God"

Chapter 21   David Sang His Prayers

Major Concept: David played music. He wrote and sang his prayers.

Key Word: hymns

Bible Story: "David Sang His Prayers" Based on 1 Samuel 16:11b–12, 16:18; 2 Samuel 5:4-5; Psalm 23 and Psalm 25

Chapter 22   I Can Sing My Prayers

Major Concept: I sing songs with my family and friends to tell God how much I love him.

Key Word: love

Story: "Kim's BIG Surprise"

UNIT SIX

I Celebrate Holy Days and Holidays

Chapter 23   All Saints Day

Major Concept: Saints help us know God's love. They show us how to love God and live as friends of Jesus.

Key Word: saint

Story: "Dressing Up as Saints"

Chapter 24   Thanksgiving Day

Major Concept: We thank God for all his blessings. We show we are thankful for the blessings that God gives us by sharing them with other people.

Key Word: thankful, blessing

Story: "The Thank-You Game"

Chapter 25   Getting Ready for Christmas

Major Concept: During Advent the friends of Jesus prepare for Christmas and look forward to celebrate the birth of Jesus.

Key Word: Advent

Bible Story: "The Angel Tells Mary Wonderful News"
Based on Luke 1:26–32, 36, 45–46

Chapter 26   We Celebrate Christmas

Major Concept: The Magi honor Jesus, the Son of God and Son of Mary. We honor Jesus in a special way during Christmas time.

Key Word: honor/Magi

Bible Story: "The Magi Visit the Baby Jesus"
Based on Matthew 2:1, 9-11

Chapter 27   Valentine's Day

Major Concept: Saint Valentine showed his love for God and for people. We are doing what Jesus told us to do when we help people and show them we love them.

Key Word: love

Story: "A Valentine's Day Hug"

Chapter 28   We Love God More and More

Major Concept: Lent is a special time of the year for our Church family. We do things that show we are growing in our love for God, for our family and for other people.

Key Word: Lent

Bible Story: "Kim Is Growing Up"

Chapter 29   We Celebrate Easter

Major Concept: At Easter the Church sings "Alleluia." We remember that Jesus is alive and is always with us.

Key Word: Easter/Alleluia

Story: "Grandpa Keeps His Promises"

Chapter 30   We Love Mary

Major Concept: We love Mary as our Mother, the Mother of all the friends of Jesus. The Church shows her love for Mary in many ways.

Key Word: Mary

Story: "Mary Loves Us"

Scope and Sequence

Ages Four and Five

INTRODUCTORY CHAPTERS

We Gather as the Friends of Jesus

INTRODUCTORY CHAPTERS FOCUS
Jesus is our friend. We have friends in religion class.

Chapter 1   **Jesus' Special Friends**
Major Concept: Jesus calls Peter, Andrew, James and John to follow him and to be his special friends.
Key Word: Bible/friends of Jesus
Bible Story: "Come, Follow Me." Based on Matthew 4:18–22

Chapter 2   **We Are Friends**
Major Concept: We gather with friends at religion class. We come together to learn about Jesus.
Key Word: friends
Story: "Be My Friend"

UNIT ONE

God Knows and Loves Us

UNIT ONE FOCUS
Jesus tells us that each person is special to God.
God loves us and cares for us.

Chapter 3   **Jesus Welcomes the Children**
Major Concept: Jesus invites the children to come to him and he blesses them. Children are special to God.
Key Word: Jesus
Bible Story: "Jesus Blesses the Children" Based on Matthew 19:13–15, Mark 10:13–16 and Luke 18:15–17

Chapter 4   **We Are Special**
Major Concept: God loves us. We are all special. Our likenesses and differences make us special, or unique, individuals.
Key Word: special/unique
Story: "Who Is God's Favorite?"

Chapter 5   **The Good Shepherd**
Major Concept: Jesus is the Good Shepherd. The sheep trust the good shepherd because he is always kind to them. He loves and cares for his sheep.
Key Word: trust
Bible Story: "Jesus Is the Good Shepherd." Based on John 10:14–15 and Luke 15:3–7

Chapter 6   **We Are Kind**
Major Concept: We show our love for one another. We are kind to one another.
Key Word: kind
Story: "Ming's Furry Puppy"

UNIT TWO

God Gave Us the World

UNIT TWO FOCUS
God created the world and everything and everyone good.
All of God's creation is a sign that God loves us.
We show our love for God by taking care of his creation.

Chapter 7   **God Made the World**
Major Concept: God is the Creator. God created the world and people good.
Key Word: creation
Bible Story: "God Made All Things Good" Based on Genesis 1:6–27

Chapter 8   **We Care for God's Creation**
Major Concept: We show our love for God by taking care of creation.
Key Word: care/caring
Story: "Ducks and Flowers"

Chapter 9   **God Always Loves Us**
Major Concept: God promises to always love and care for Noah, his family, and for all people. The rainbow in the sky is a sign of God's promise.
Key Word: promise
Bible Story: "God's Promise" Based on Genesis 6—9

Chapter 10   **We Love Others**
Major Concept: God always shares his love with us. We show our love for others when we share with them.
Key Word: share
Story: "Only One Cookie"

UNIT THREE

Jesus Is God's Own Son

UNIT THREE FOCUS
God sent Jesus, his own Son, to us. Mary and Joseph loved and cared for Jesus. Our families love us and care for us.

Chapter 11   **Jesus Is Born**
Major Concept: Jesus was born to Mary. Jesus is Mary's Son and God's own Son.
Key Word: Mary
Bible Story: "Mary's Baby" Based on Luke 1:26–35, 2:1–7, 15–17

Chapter 12   **We Celebrate Jesus' Birthday**
Major Concept: We celebrate the birth of Jesus with joy. We celebrate the birth of Jesus with our family and all the friends of Jesus.
Key Word: celebrate
Story: "The Christmas Play"

Chapter 13   **Jesus Belonged to a Family**
Major Concept: Jesus, Mary and Joseph are the Holy Family. Jesus lived in a family who loved and cared for him.
Key Word: Holy Family
Bible Story: "The Boy Jesus in the Temple" Based on Luke 2:41–52

Chapter 14   **We Belong to a Family**
Major Concept: We are a part of a family who loves and cares for us.
Key Word: belong
Story: "A Family's Love"

The Stories of God's Love Kids

CARLOS

Hi. My name is Carlos.
I love trucks.
I live with my Mom and Dad.
My favorite color is blue.

Carlos is a very active, happy little boy. He is smiling all the time. He spends time with his dad while his mom is at work. Carlos also loves to go to the park with his Grandpa. He loves Grandpa very much. When he grows up he wants to be a truck driver.

KIM

Hi. My name is Kim.
I love music and want to play the drums.
I like to play by myself sometimes.
My favorite color is red.

Kim lives with her parents and grandparents. She also has a baby sister names Mya. Her aunt and uncle live in China. Sometimes Kim is quite and likes to listen to music. She wants to play the drums when she grows up.

ABBY

Hi. My name is Abby.
I like to help my Mom.
I have lots of dolls.
My favorite color is orange.

Abby lives with her Mom in an apartment, but Grandma and Grandpa come to visit sometimes. She loves to play with her dolls, and she is very kind to them. Abby wants to be a mom when she grows up.

JAMAL

Hi. My name is Jamal.
I live on a farm.
I like to dig in the dirt.
My favorite color is green.

Jamal lives with his mom and dad. They live on a farm so he loves to help his dad plant seeds. Jamal has lots of questions and loves to learn. When he grows up he wants to be a farmer. He loves to visit his Grandpa.

Component Overview

Children's Leaflets

Program Director's Manual

Catechist/Teacher Guides

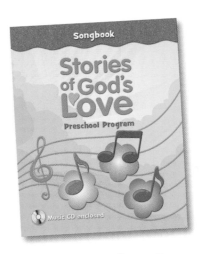

Songbook

Teaching Posters

Music CD

Children's Leaflets

There are 30 story-based leaflets for each level of *Stories of God's Love:*

- Two introductory lessons to welcome the children.
- Ten Bible story lessons.
- Ten present-day life story lessons that connect with the Scripture stories.
- Eight seasonal celebrations.

Scripture stories form the heart of the *Stories of God's Love* Preschool Religion Readiness Program. Young children are introduced to a new Bible Story of God's love from the Scriptures every other week. A corresponding Life Story related to the child's life reinforces the Scriptural theme is presented on alternate weeks.

Week 1: Bible Story

The Bible Story presents the faith theme of the lesson.

Week 2: Life Story

The Life Story parallels the Bible Story theme from the previous week and connects the faith theme to the child's every day life.

Character Punch-outs

ABBY

CARLOS

KIM

JAMAL

Set of character punch-outs for child to use for storytelling and other activities

Certificate

Colorful diploma for each child recognizing their participation in the program

18

Activity Pages

The center spread of each leaflet contains an engaging activity to help the children apply and integrate the weekly session theme into their own lives.

For My Family Page

A resource that supports parent's efforts to actively participate in the faith development of their child

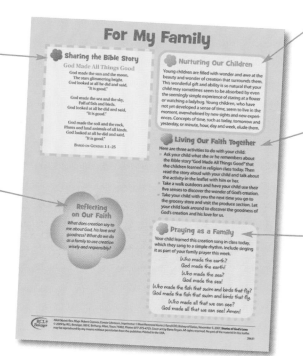

Sharing the Story

The story told in class is provided for the parents for retelling at home.

Reflecting on Our Faith

A question invites parents to reflect on the ways the faith theme intersects with their own personal and family life.

Nurturing Our Children

Advice from experts gives parents tips regarding their child's development.

Living Our Faith Together

A variety of activities to foster integrating what the children have learned into everyday family life.

Praying as a Family

Weekly family prayers provide parents ways to guide their children in developing good prayer habits.

Seasonal Lessons

Each level of *Stories of God's Love* provides eight seasonal lessons that:

- introduce children to holy days, holidays, feasts and liturgical seasons.
- build Catholic identity.
- provide stories, activities, and prayers.
- offer ways to extend the celebrations into the home.

- All Saints' Day
- Thanksgiving
- Advent
- Christmas

- Valentine's Day
- Lent
- Easter
- Mary

Additional Resources

Music Program

Music is an integral part of *Stories of God's Love*. The music program includes the following elements:

- Music CD containing both lyrics and instrumental versions of each song
- Songbook with lyrics and accompaniment for piano and guitar and a prayer celebration for each unit

Teaching Posters

Stories of God's Love provides you with a teaching poster for every session. These provide a focal point for story time. The posters contain the same images and story as the ones on the corresponding Children's Leaflet.

RCLBenzigerPreschool.com

Go to *RCLBenzigerPreschool.com* to find a multitude of ideas for teachers and parents to help young children take their first steps in faith. You'll find additional activities, and teaching tips, as well as our unique feature, "Ask an Expert," where you can type in any question you may have about your work as a teacher and receive a prompt reply.

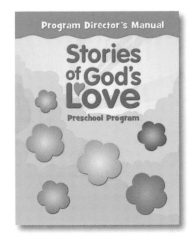

Program Director's Manual

Preschool Program Coordinators will find a treasury of resources in this manual to support their teachers and parents and to connect the religion readiness program to the whole community of faith.

Guide

Background Page

Chapter background information to assist the catechist in preparing for the chapter theme that includes:

Background for the Catechist

A brief scriptural and theological reflection related to the chapter faith theme

For Reflection

A question inviting teachers to reflect on their living of the chapter faith theme and their modeling the faith theme for the children

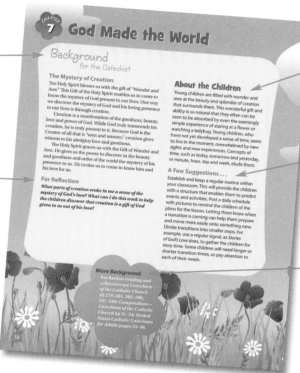

About the Children

Insights into the development of preschool-age children

A Few Suggestions

Practical teaching tips for effective and age-appropriate lessons

More Background

References to the *Catechism of the Catholic Church, Compendium: Catechism of the Catholic Church* and *United States Catholic Catechism for Adults*

Lesson Planner

Faith Focus

The major faith focus for the chapter

Enriching the Lesson

A quick reminder for additional resources to enrich the lesson with song and the variety of opportunities on RCLBenzigerPreschool.com

Chapter Objectives

Brief statement of lesson objectives to guide your teaching

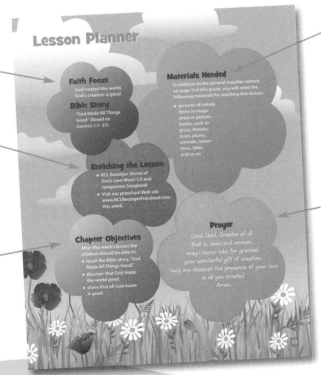

Materials Needed

A detailed list of necessary materials to complete the lesson

Prayer

A prayer centered on the session theme to prepare the teacher

Lesson Plan

In *Stories of God's Love* you will follow this easy to use step-by-step process as you teach each lesson:

- Welcome and Gather
- Teach and Apply
- Pray

Welcome

Each chapter begins with a hands-on activity that introduces the children to the theme of the chapter.

Gather

Music signals the children to move from the Welcome Center to the Story Time Area and helps focus them on the chapter story.

Teach

In every lesson the children discover and learn through story. (1) The story is introduced and the children are given a purpose for listening. (2) The children listen to the story. (3) The children are guided to recall the details of the story to reinforce their knowledge of the story.

Prayer

Your lessons end in prayer. Additional extended prayer celebrations are provided in the *Stories of God's Love Song* Book.

Apply

Age-appropriate activities engage the children that reinforce their understanding of the story and connect what they have learned to their everyday life.

Additional Activities

Optional activities are provided in every chapter. They offer you choices for class activities that include strategies for the many ways children learn.

Activity Masters

Reproducible masters are provided throughout to enhance the activities.

Getting Ready

The Environment as the Third Teacher

Young children learn from active exploration of their environment. It is important that we think about setting up the classroom with activity centers that allow children to explore and learn.

Preschoolers generally do not sit quietly at a table or floor activity for very long (8–10 minutes maximum). Thus, the environment needs to be designed to allow them to move around, be active, and make choices. Teachers can "play" with the children, guiding them to engage in tasks that help the children learn the concept of the day, such as "caring for others" or "Jesus wants me to be kind to my friends."

Refer to the Program Director's Manual or series Web site for suggested materials and centers. Establishing an appropriate and engaging environment will take some planning on the teacher's part. However, these efforts can pay off with young children who are engaged in learning.

The Importance of Active Learning and Enticing Materials

Children at this stage of development learn by interacting with the materials and activities. Thus, the teacher will need to plan ahead to have enticing materials (those that make the child want to participate) set up in an inviting and engaging manner. It is best if children are allowed to explore the materials so that they can make their own meaning with the guidance of the teacher. Modeling activities can be helpful, but remember that children at this age may not get it "right" or have their product look like yours. The learning is what is important through active engagement.

Classroom Management through Guiding Behavior

Positive behavior management techniques have been proven to be more effective than punitive or negative management strategies. Strategies that will help decrease behavior problems include being ready for class (having all your materials ready, music and books ready to go), praising appropriate behavior (sharing, helping others, picking up toys or trash) and having a daily routine with cues to the children when it is time for a transition and what the next activity will be. Guiding children through verbal prompts, modeling of appropriate behavior and praising acts of kindness and acts of helping will all encourage children to "behave" in class.

You will also need to support the children as they learn to manage conflicts. Help them learn the words and support them as they practice using them.

Getting Ready

Health and Safety First!

Little children are infamous for runny noses, coughing, and sharing their germs! You can help stop the spreading of germs by encouraging and modeling appropriate hand washing with soap after using the restroom, before eating snacks, or after participating in a particularly messy activity. Having tissues handy and teaching children to "cover your mouth" in the crook of their arm will also be helpful.

Safety also needs to be taught, with gentle reminders of class/school rules (no running in the hallways, no climbing or sitting on furniture other than chairs, no hitting, and so on). It is often helpful for the children to be involved in making the rules, with the teacher writing them on poster board and the children decorating the poster once it is complete.

Appropriate tools need to be available for the children to use, including safety scissors (round tips), non-toxic washable paints and crayons, and child-size tools if using any for the weekly activities. Medical issues and allergies need to be known about the children, as does emergency contact information for the parents/caregiver.

Family Involvement and Communication

Encourage families to be involved in the program. They can help in the classroom, use the Children's Leaflet to practice new concepts at home or donate materials that are listed on the classroom wish list (see the Program Director's Manual and Web site).

The parents' role may be somewhat different with this age group as separation is often difficult for children until they begin to trust the teacher. Parents should be encouraged to stay and join in with the lesson until their child is comfortable. Gradually they should be able to leave the child for longer and longer periods of time as the children adjust to their new surroundings.

Parents should be encouraged to view the family page of the Children's Leaflet and to read the Bible and life stories presented and discuss the topics of the lesson also included for family discussion. Taking a few minutes to talk with the parents as they drop off or pick up the children will help make transitions smoother for the children and will let the parents be aware of what their child did while at school.

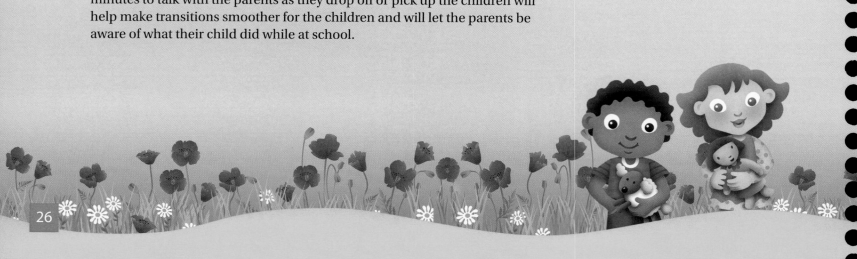

Working with Children with Special Learning Needs and Developmental Differences

Children with special learning needs are likely to be members of your class and can be accommodated with some basic modifications. Most children with special needs, including children with autism, learn best through repetition, consistency (schedule, locations in the room for specific events such as Bible/story time, prayer table, and so on), cues for attention (calling their name before asking a question, telling the class to listen for a particular concept as you are reading, or seating them next to you for quick taps on the shoulder or knee to help them refocus on you), and visual cues (pictures, models, word cards, or sequencing cards to complete a task).

Children with visual impairments benefit from enlarged materials, physical cues such as outlining a picture with a line of glue that will harden and leave a ridge, and verbal descriptions of what the other children are seeing to help them learn and participate in given tasks.

Children who are deaf or hard of hearing generally benefit from sitting where they can see the speaker's lips, visual cues, and possibly an amplification system. Physical impairments can be accommodated by room arrangement, seating of the other children in the class (others in chairs instead of sitting on the floor if the child needs to stay seated in a wheelchair), and modified utensils and tools that can be provided by the family or child's therapists.

Children who are gifted or talented also need to be considered. Provide enrichment activities to keep them interested in the tasks and activities.

Resources to Use with the Children

Introductory Unit

First Day by Joan Rankin (Margaret K. McElderry 2002)

Theme: welcome, parent-child relationship

Haybillybun struggles with the first day of preschool while his mother worries at home about whether he will be okay.

First Friends by Lenore Blegvad (HarperFestival, 2000)

Theme: friendship, sharing

Through object identification, word repetition and rhyme, the reader explores the environment of a preschool classroom through the eyes of a preschool child.

That's What Friends Are For by Valeri Gorbachev (Philomel, 2005)

Theme: friendship

In this fourth book in a series, Goat and Pig experience the meaning of friendship when Goat misunderstands Pig's tears from cutting onions which turns into an opportunity for them to make and enjoy dinner together.

Wemberly Worried by Kevin Henkes (Live Oak Media, 2001)

Theme: welcome, friendship

Wemberly, a little girl mouse, worries about everything small and big until she meets new friends on the first day of preschool.

Unit One

A Stormy Ride on Noah's Ark by Patricia Hooper (Putnam Juvenile, 2001)

Theme: trust

The traditional Old Testament story is told through rhyming verse focusing on the animals overcoming their fear of the storm by trusting in Noah.

Because of You by B. G. Hennessy (Candlewick, 2005)

Theme: kindness, friendship, peace

This book highlights the importance of the individual and how each of us can make a difference in the world through our sharing and helping others.

Elinor and Violet: Two Naughty Chickens at the Beach by Patti Beling Murphy (Amazon Remainders Account, 2003)

Theme: trust

Elinor and Violet take their hilarious troublesome adventures to the beach, where Elinor must decide what is the right thing to do.

Henry and Amy: Right-Way-Round and Upside Down by Stephen Michael King (Walker & Company, 1999)

Theme: uniqueness

Henry and Amy might have very different personalities, but the two complement each other well in this story about how friends who are different can learn from each other.

How Kind! by Mary Murphy (Walker Books Ltd, 2004)

Theme: kindness

Happy barn animals Hen and Pig exchange gifts which leads to a chain reaction of other acts of kindness on the farm.

In the Moonlight, Waiting by Carol Carrick (Clarion Books, 1990)

Theme: shepherd, sheep

A young girl and her little brother welcome a new-born lamb, and then the little girl stays awake watching the ewe, waiting for the possibility of another new baby lamb.

Little Baa by Kim Lewis (Walker Books Ltd, 2004)

Theme: shepherd, sheep, mother and child

A lost lamb and his mother are reunited by a young shepherd and his dog.

Mary Had a Little Lamb by Sarah Josepha Hale (Orchard Books, 2000)

Theme: shepherd, sheep

In this new interpretation of the classic children's nursery rhyme, the familiar characters of Mary, her family, teacher, friends and lamb are illustrated through fabric relief.

Otis by Janie Bynum (Voyager Books, 2003)

Theme: uniqueness, friendship

Otis is a young pig who dislikes the mud. He eventually befriends a young frog who also does not care to be dirty by mud.

The First Thing My Mama Told Me by Susan Marie Swanson (Harcourt Children's Books, 2002)

Theme: names

On her seventh birthday, Lucy fondly reflects back on the joyous memories she has about her name.

The Kindness Quilt by Nancy Elizabeth Wallace (Marshall Cavendish Corporation, 2006)

Theme: kindness

Minna, a young rabbit, and her friends learn about acts of kindness when their teacher, Mrs. Bloom, assigns them a kindness project. So Minna decides to make a quilt to illustrate the various acts of kindness she performed.

Toot and Puddle: You Are My Sunshine by Hobbie, Holly (Little, Brown, 2001)

Theme: friendship

Friends of Toot try to cheer him up from his gloominess and sorrow. After some time and a storm, Toot finally gains a new outlook because of the support of his friends.

Where is the Green Sheep? by Mem Fox (Chrysalis Children's Books, 2005)

Theme: shepherd, sheep

Children will discover various types of sheep through easy rhyme, color recognition and repetition.

Unit Two

Because Your Daddy Loves You by Andrew Clements (Clarion Books, 2005)

Theme: caring for ourselves, parent/child relationship

This book celebrates a father's unconditional love and patience for his daughter who experiences some frustration while at the beach.

Good Job, Little Bear! by Martin Waddell (Candlewick, 2002)

Theme: caring for ourselves, parent/child relationship

Big Bear and Little Bear are on an expedition together where Little Bear explores his surroundings closely supported by his loving father, Big Bear.

Resources to Use with the Children

It's MY Birthday! By Pat Hutchins (Greenwillow, 1999)

Theme: sharing

Billy, the young green monster, is back for his birthday where receiving gifts becomes a difficult lesson in learning how to share.

Maisy's Wonderful Weather Book by Lucy Cousins (Candlewick, 2006)

Theme: God's wondrous creation

Whatever the weather, Maisy has fun, and so too the reader with the pull-tabs and flaps to help forecast the weather with Maisy.

Noah's Trees by Bijou Le Tord (HarperCollins Children's Books, 2007)

Theme: caring for God's creation

In this new perspective on the Old Testament story, Noah is a gardener who tends to dozens of trees. When God asks Noah to build the ark, he does so obediently, making sure to take pairs of animals and plenty of saplings along.

One for Me, One for You by C.C. Cameron (Roaring Brook Press, 2003)

Theme: sharing

Two friends, a hippo and alligator, learn about counting and sharing their cookies and toys.

Rain by Manya Stojic (Chrysalis Children's Books, 2001)

Theme: God's wondrous creation

Follow the animals of the African savanna who eagerly anticipate and experience rain through the senses of smell, sight, sound, touch and taste.

The Way I Love You by David Bedford (Simon & Schuster Children's Publishing, 2004)

Theme: caring for God's creation

A young girl counts the ways she and her dog are best friends.

Unit Three

A Child was Born: A First Nativity Book by Grace Maccarone (Scholastic, 2000)

Theme: Christmas

The story of the birth of Jesus is told through short rhyming sentences.

Bubba and Beau Meet the Relatives by Kathi Appelt (Harcourt Children's Books, 2004)

Theme: family

The hilarious adventures of Bubba and Beau continue when Granddaddy Bubba, Grandma Ruby, Aunt Sapphire, Cousin Arlene and dog Bitsy visit.

Full, Full, Full of Love by Trish Cooke (Walker Books, 2004)

Theme: family

In this tribute to extended families, Jay Jay spends a day with Grannie who keeps him busy helping prepare a feast for the whole family.

The Boy Who Longed for a Lift by Norma Farber (HarperCollins, 1997)

Theme: family

A young boy who runs away from home eventually returns to the loving embrace of his father.

We Have a Baby by Cathryn Falwell (Clarion Books, 1999)

Theme: family

A family celebrates the arrival of a new baby.

Welcome, Precious by Nikki Grimes (Orchard Books, 2006)

Theme: family

This poetic illustration joyously highlights an African American family welcoming the newest member of the family.

Who Was Born This Special Day? by Eve Bunting (Aladdin, 2003)

Theme: Christmas

This holiday bedtime story presents the birth of Jesus from a contemplative perspective of those animals present by the manger.

Unit Four

Simon and Molly Plus Hester by Lisa Jahn-Clough (Houghton Mifflin/Walter Lorraine Books, 2001)

Theme: friendship

Simon and Molly are best friends, and then Molly befriends Hester, causing Simon to feel left out. So the three work through reconciling the friendships.

That's What Friends Are For by Valeri Gorbachev (Philomel, 2005)

Theme: friendship

In this fourth book in a series, Goat and Pig experience the meaning of friendship when Goat misunderstands Pig's tears from cutting onions which turns into an opportunity for them to make and enjoy dinner together.

Toot and Puddle: You Are My Sunshine by Holly Hobbie (Little Brown, 2001)

Theme: friendship

Friends of Toot try to cheer him up from his gloominess and sorrow. After some time and a storm, Toot finally gains a new outlook because of the support of his friends.

We Go to Mass by Judy Winkler (Catholic Book Publishing Company, 2004)

Theme: Mass, church

This book contains a creative way to help the children learn about the Mass with five exciting jigsaw puzzles alongside a description for the major parts of the Mass.

What Game Shall We Play? by Pat Hutchins (Harper Trophy, 1995)

Theme: friendship

Duck and Frog seek out their animal friends for a game to play. Eventually Owl suggests the game of hide-and-seek.

Unit Five

Barnyard Prayers by Laura Godwin (Hyperion, 2000)

Theme: prayers

A young boy imagines that he is a farmer and his toy animals come to life. Through a series of prayers, each animal prays to God according to his nature.

God Bless Me, God Bless You by Lois Rock (Baker Book House, 2001)

Theme: prayer

In a style of bedtime prayers, a young boy and girl pray to God for the people, animals and things in their life.

How Does God Listen? by Kay Lindahl (Skylight Paths Publishing, 2005)

Theme: prayer

Young readers will explore spiritual questions that speak to their heart. The children learn that God's presence can be experienced through the use of their senses.

Resources to Use with the Children

My Book of Thanks by B. G. Hennessy (Candlewick, 2005)

Theme: prayer

A collection of prayers and petitions for young children to enjoy.

Sing a New Song: A Book of Psalms by Bijou Le Tord (Wm. B. Eerdmans Publishing Company, 1997)

Theme: prayer

A beautiful collection of psalm verses combined with equally beautiful watercolor illustrations.

Unit Six

1, 2, 3, Valentine's Day by Jeanne Modesitt (Boyds Mills Press, 2002)

Theme: Valentine's Day

In this rhyming counting book that celebrates the love of Valentine's Day, Mister Mouse, dressed in a dark pink suit, visits his animal friends to give them gifts.

A Child was Born: A First Nativity Book by Grace Maccarone (Scholastic, 2000)

Theme: Christmas

The story of the birth of Jesus is told through short rhyming sentences.

In My Heart by Molly Bang (Little Brown Young Readers, 2006)

Theme: motherhood

With a cast of multicultural characters, a mother describes the love in her heart for her child as she reflects on all the aspects of her day.

Mommy's Hands by Kathryn Lasky and Jane Kamine (Hyperion, 2002)

Theme: motherhood

The love of a mother for her child is affectionately described through the daily actions of her hands.

My Book of Thanks by B. G. Hennessy (Candlewick, 2005)

Theme: prayer

A collection of prayers and petitions for young children to enjoy.

My Mom by Anthony Browne (Farrar, Straus and Giroux, 2005)

Theme: motherhood

This book is an affectionate tribute to motherhood from the perspective of the adoring child with illustrations of the everyday mom who is the strongest woman in the world.

Over the River and through the Wood by Lydia Maria Child and Iris Van Rynbach (Little Brown & Co., 1989)

Theme: thanksgiving

Full-page illustrations detail rural scenes alongside this familiar children's poem about a visit to grandmother's house on Thanksgiving Day.

Saint Francis and the Christmas Donkey by Robert Byrd (Dutton Juvenile, 2000)

Theme: All Saints Day

Saint Francis meets a donkey in the forest who is struggling with all of the heavy burden he carries every day. Saint Francis tells him the story of the birth of Jesus which raises his spirits.

A Catechist's Prayer

Gracious God, I ask your blessing as I begin this year
as a catechist to the young children in our preschool program.
Help me follow the example of your Son, Jesus, and all faithful
people as I help these young ones take their first steps in faith.

Give me the spirit of *welcome* that Jesus showed
when he gathered children around him. Remind me to show
the preschool children how much I appreciate the blessing
that each of them brings to our class.

Give me the gift of *persistence* displayed by the Good Shepherd
who cared for each of his sheep. Help me give special attention
to the children who most need to know your love for them.

Give me the spirit of *love* present in the Holy Family.
Guide me in creating a circle of love and mutual respect
within my teaching space.

Give me the gift of *faith* of the first disciples, who answered Jesus'
call to proclaim his Good News to all people. May I tell the stories
of your great love for us with the same passion and commitment.

Give me the spirit of *forgiveness* as I teach the children to be
thoughtful and to forgive one another as your Son taught us to do.

Above all, help me to create a community of faith which is marked
by listening, sharing, praising you, and treating one another with
a spirit of love and care. Instill in me a child's sense of wonder
and awe as I reflect on the mystery of your love and on the gift
of being invited to serve as your catechist this year. Amen.

CHAPTER 1 Jesus Welcomes the Children

Background
for the Catechist

Growing in Faith

The Bible story for today's session is found in the Gospels of Matthew, Mark and Luke. In this story, people are pressing toward Jesus with their children but are rebuked by the disciples. Jesus, however, calls to the children and says, "Let the children come to me and do not prevent them; for the [K]ingdom of God belongs to such as these. Amen, I say to you, whoever does not accept the [K]ingdom of God like a child will not enter it" (Luke 18:16–17).

So what does it mean to accept the Kingdom of God like a child? It means that we have a faith that is rooted in complete trust and abandonment to God's will. As a child looks with complete and total trust in those who care for them that they will be well protected and loved, so too are we called to such a level of trust and faith in God.

Jesus constantly calls us to deeper faith in his Father and reminds us that God is aware of all of our needs and is always providing for us. Jesus' very life is a model of trust in God the Father who is always reaching out to us with love.

For Reflection

In what ways can I become more childlike in faith? How might my actions and my own faith build trust with the children I am working with this week?

About the Children

The way we welcome children into our classrooms is very important. Our greetings and smiles will tell the children how much we enjoy being with them. As we welcome the children, it is also important to give a special welcome to their parents or caregivers. Invite them to stay in the classroom for part of the lesson or for the whole lesson. Share with the children that they can meet other new friends and do a fun activity in the Welcome Center. Take the time to explain the activity to both the children and their parents. Your joy and enthusiasm for helping these young children learn about God will encourage them to want to participate in the lessons.

A Few Suggestions . . .

One way we create a positive relationship with each of the children is by bending or kneeling down to their eye level to greet them. Ask each child to tell you something they enjoy doing, and share with them some fun things they will be doing in religion class. Encourage the parents or caregivers to help them make their name badges, and always share that you welcome their presence in the classroom.

More Background

For further reading and reflection see *Catechism of the Catholic Church* §§ 163–165, 301, 305; *Compendium—Catechism of the Catholic Church* § 27; *United States Catholic Catechism for Adults* pages 37, 44, 59.

Lesson Planner

Faith Focus

Jesus welcomes all children.

Bible Story

"Let the Children Come to Me" (Based on Matthew 19:13–15, Mark 10:13–16 and Luke 18:15–17)

Enriching the Lesson

- RCL Benziger *Stories of God's Love* Music CD and companion Songbook, Song 1
- Visit our preschool Web site www.RCLBenzigerPreschool.com this week.

Materials Needed

In addition to the general supplies named on page 9 of this guide, you will need the following materials for teaching this lesson:

- name badge for each child made from stiff poster board cut into rectangles with edges rounded-off for safety
- several washable markers of different colors
- glue and collage material or stickers for children to use to decorate name badges
- yarn to make name-badge necklaces
- closed Bible with bookmark placed at Matthew 19:13–15

Chapter Objectives

After this week's lesson the children should be able to:

- recall the Bible story "Let the Children Come to Me."
- recognize that Jesus loves them.
- share with their family that Jesus loves them.

Prayer

God, Father of all,
you welcome us into your embrace
as Jesus welcomed the children.
Help me to grow in faith
so that I may share my faith and trust
in your great love
with the children in my care.
Amen.

1 Jesus Welcomes the Children

Stories of God's Love
Ages 3 and 4

Let the Children Come to Me

Many people came to Jesus to listen to him. One day some people brought their children to Jesus. They wanted their children to be close to Jesus.

Some of Jesus' special friends and helpers told the people to stay back. They told them not to let the children get too close to Jesus and not to bother him.

When Jesus saw and heard what his helpers were doing, he stopped them and said, "Let the children come to me. Children are very special to God and close to him. You need to love and trust God as children do."

Jesus took the children into his arms, put his hands on them and blessed them.

BASED ON MATTHEW 19:13–15,
MARK 10:13–16 AND LUKE 18:15–17

Welcome

- Set up a Welcome Center each week. Include enticing materials that relate to the story for the week. This week provide fun art materials that the children can use to make or decorate a name badge.
- Bend or kneel down and greet the children as they enter. Introduce yourself and show the children your name badge. Direct the children to the Welcome Center and invite them to choose a marker for you or their parents to use to write their name in large letters on the name badge and then to decorate their name badge.
- Encourage the children to share the materials, and acknowledge children who display cooperative behavior with such statements as, "Sara, thank you for passing the green crayon to Nick."
- Assist the children in completing their name badges by punching holes in the corners of the name badges and using yarn to make name-badge necklaces that the children can place around their necks.

Gather

- As children begin to finish their work in the Welcome Center, begin to softly play song 1, the theme song, provided on the *Stories of God's Love* Music CD or another gathering song that you will regularly use to signal that it is time for the children to clean up and move to the Story Time Area.
- Encourage the children to tidy up the Welcome Center and help others if needed.
- Invite the children to the Story Time Area wearing their name-badge necklaces.

Teach

Introduce the Bible story.

- Sing the following welcome song to help the children learn one another's names to the tune of "Skip to My Lou," or create your own tune. Repeat the song until you have welcomed each child.

   Hello *(child's name)*. We're glad you're here!
   Hello *(child's name)*. We're glad you're here!
   Hello *(child's name)*. We're glad you're here!
      Welcome to our class.

- Collect the name badges. Place them near the door for the children to pick up as they leave or save them for the next gathering.
- Show the children a Bible. Share with them that the Bible is a very special book that God gave us. The Bible is the holy book of our Church family. The Bible tells us many stories about God's love for us.
- Show the children the illustration on the teaching poster or the children's leaflet. Point to and name Jesus. Tell the children that Jesus told us the best stories about God's

love. Invite the children to listen closely to what Jesus told the children.

Tell the Bible story.

Invite a child to come up and open the Bible to the place marked by the bookmark, Matthew 19:13–15. Take the opened Bible, place the children's leaflet inside. Tell the children the name of the Bible story "Let the Children Come to Me." Refer to the teaching poster or the cover of the children's leaflet as you read the Bible story on the For My Family Page to the children.

Recall the Bible story.

- Tell the children that you will play a game with them to help them remember the Bible story. Explain that you are going to say something from the Bible story but are going to leave out an important word. They will say the missing word. Model the activity. For example, while pointing to your shirt: I am wearing a _____. *(shirt)*
  — The people brought their _____ to see Jesus. *(children)*
  — The friends of Jesus told the people to _____. *(stay back)*
  — Jesus said, "Let the _____ come to me." *(children)*
  — Jesus took the children into his _____ and blessed them. *(arms)*
- Summarize by reminding the children that Jesus loves them as he loved the children in the Bible story.

 Apply

Work on the children's leaflet activity.

- Distribute the children's leaflet. Give the children time to look at them. Talk about the different parts of the leaflet, explaining to them that the back page has a special message for their family.
- Call their attention to the picture on the center two pages and ask them to describe what they see. *(Children marching with flags.)* Tell them that the names of the children in the picture are Carlos, Kim, Abby and Jamal.
- Ask the children to listen carefully as you tell them what the flags say. *(Jesus loves all children.)* Have them color the

Jesus Loves Me
Jesus Loves ALL Children
Color the flags.
Tell Jesus, "I am glad to be your friend."

flags. Read all the words aloud together after they have completed the activity.

Connect with the child's life.

- Talk about how happy we are that we have the Bible so that we can hear stories about Jesus. Remind the children that today our Bible story told us Jesus loved the children. Point out to the children that the story also tells us that Jesus loves them. Encourage the children to tell their family, "Jesus loves me and Jesus loves you too!"
- Tell the children to take their leaflet home and share the Bible story on the For My Family Page and the activity with their family.

Pray

- Gather the children at the prayer table. Tell them that you will teach them a special prayer that they will say to begin their prayer at the end of religion class. Teach them: "My head I bow. / My hands I fold. / Now I talk to God." Note: Use this call to silence to prepare the children for prayer throughout the year.
- Introduce today's prayer by saying, "Today we will thank Jesus for loving the children and for loving us." Practice the prayer with the children.

  Teacher: Thank you, Jesus, for loving the children.
  Children: Thank you, Jesus, for loving the children.
  Teacher: Thank you, Jesus, for loving me.
  Children: Thank you, Jesus, for loving me.
  Teacher: Together let us pray, "Amen."
  All: Amen.

- Tell the children to quiet themselves for prayer as they quietly pray in their hearts "My head I bow . . ." *(Pause.)*
- Lead the children in prayer.

Additional Activities

Tell the Bible story using blocks.
Use this activity to help the children recall the Bible story.
- Tape the *Stories of God's Love* children punch-out figures to blocks to make stand-up figures.
- Put these figures and some additional blocks in the Story Time Area.
- Have the children use the figures to retell the Bible story.

Share your favorite things.
Use this activity to help the children share about themselves.
- Fold a piece of plain white paper into four sections.
- Write "My Favorite Things" on the top of the page.
- Invite the children to draw pictures of one of their favorite things in each square.
- Give assistance to children who need help.

CHAPTER 2 My Teacher Welcomes Me

Background
for the Catechist

Friends of Jesus

In the second part of the Great Commandment, Jesus calls us to love our neighbors as ourselves. (See Matthew 22:39.) When we love others as ourselves, our relationships with other people are characterized by caring, helping, sharing and communicating.

Jesus showed us the importance of communication with others as a basis of friendship. He told his disciples, "I have called you friends, because I have told you everything I have heard from my Father" (John 15:15). Good communication is the foundation for any strong relationship.

We have been called together by God to be his Church, the community of the friends of Jesus Christ. We care about and for one another. We help one another. We share our material and spiritual blessings with one another. Together we experience, celebrate and communicate the love of Christ to all of those around us.

For Reflection

In what ways do I live out the call to love others as myself? What can I do to help the children reach out to others as friends?

About the Children

Three- and young four-year-olds use their growing mastery of language to engage with their environment and the people in their environment. They employ an increasing number of speech patterns that initiate and keep conversations going with others. Their growing awareness of self and others will enable them to begin to play simple games and participate for longer periods of time in small-group experiences. Most threes and young fours will enjoy sitting and listening to engaging stories for up to ten minutes but still need ample opportunities to move, interact and play with others.

A Few Suggestions . . .

Sharing and listening are key skills necessary for the development of social relationships. Modeling these skills and giving young children ample opportunities to practice them is important and can help children build new friendships with peers and adults. By asking children for their input and really listening to their responses, you will help children both learn how to engage in conversation and feel good about their contribution. Incorporating moments when children share with each other what they like or what they have done can begin to build the foundation for good listening skills.

More Background

For further reading and reflection see *Catechism of the Catholic Church* §§ 748–757, 787–789; *Compendium—Catechism of the Catholic Church* §§ 147–160; *United States Catholic Catechism for Adults* pages 111–123.

Lesson Planner

Faith Focus

We gather as friends to learn about Jesus who welcomes us to be his friends.

Story

"Jamal and Abby"

Materials Needed

In addition to the general supplies named on page 9 of this guide, you will need the following materials for teaching this lesson:

- paper in variety of colors, weights and textures (construction paper, copy paper, card stock, sand paper) cut into the shapes of circles, squares, triangles and rectangles
- medium-sized soft ball
- punch-out figures of Jamal and Abby

Enriching the Lesson

- RCL Benziger *Stories of God's Love* Music CD and companion Songbook, Song 1
- Visit our preschool Web site www.RCLBenzigerPreschool.com this week.

Chapter Objectives

After this week's lesson the children should be able to:

- recall the story "Jamal and Abby."
- name some things that Jamal and Abby like about their religion class.
- share things they like to do in religion class.

Prayer

Lord God,
I love you with
all my heart, soul and mind.
Help me reach out in love to others,
welcoming all as friends.
May my example help encourage the children
to do the same.
Amen.

Jamal and Abby

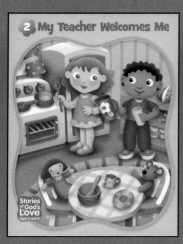

Jamal tucked the fluffy yellow blanket around the baby doll in the toy bed. He was having so much fun playing in the family center during religion class. Abby was in the center with him. She was pretending to cook soup on the play stove.

Abby looked at Jamal and said, "I love to play pretend in the family center. Miss Diaz said we could play here for a little while longer. I'm going to make soup and lemonade for the dolls. Want to help me?"

Jamal smiled at his new friend and said, "Yum! I wish the lemonade was real. It's my favorite!"

Abby giggled and said, "It's just pretend, silly."

"I know," he answered. "I like to pretend. I like to come to religion class so we can play together. What is your favorite thing here?"

"Ummm . . . I like Miss Diaz. She is so nice. And I like the way she tells us stories about Jesus," Abby said.

"Me too!" Jamal said. "And you know what Miss Diaz said? She said Jesus loves all of us!"

Abby smiled as she stirred her pretend soup. Stories about Jesus made her feel good inside. She wanted Miss Diaz to tell them more about Jesus. Abby couldn't wait to tell her Mom all about her new friend Jamal and the stories about Jesus Miss Diaz told them.

 ## Welcome

- Provide crayons or markers; and paper of a variety of colors, weights and textures cut into shapes of squares, circles, rectangles and triangles large enough for the children to draw on. Note: Have the children wear their name-badge necklaces that they made in the previous session.
- Greet the children by name. Direct them to the Welcome Center and invite them to use the crayons and markers to draw and color a picture of something they like to do.
- Walk among the children as they are working. Address the children by name and invite them to talk about their favorite colors as they work on their drawings. Help the children get to know each other through conversation as they work, addressing one another by name.

 ## Gather

- Play the gathering song that the children first heard last week to signal that it is time for the children to clean up and move to the Story Time Area. Have the children bring their pictures to the Story Time Area. After all the children have gathered in the Story Time Area, invite them to share their pictures or talk about who they played with during the welcome time.
- Tell the children that they are going to play a game that will help everyone get to know each other. Have them stand, hold hands to form one large circle and sit back down.
- Explain to the children that you are going to call out one of their names and roll a ball to that child, saying, "(Name), welcome to our religion class." Tell them that they will keep playing the game until everyone's name has been called out and the ball rolled to them.
- Begin playing the game.

 ## Teach

Introduce the story.

- Show the children the teaching poster or the cover of the children's leaflet for chapter 2. Ask the children:
    —What do you think Jamal and Abby are doing? *(playing pretend at the family center)*
    —What might they be saying to each other? *(talking about their pretend play and their favorite thing in religion class)*
- Invite the children to listen carefully to discover what Jamal and Abby like about religion class.

Tell the story.

Tell the children the name of the story "Jamal and Abby." Tell the story using the punch-outs of Jamal and Abby to dramatize the dialog and actions of the story.

Recall the story.

Ask the children to raise both hands if they know the answers to the questions you ask them.

—Introduce Jamal and Abby once again using the punch-out figures. Refer to the brief description of each of the *Stories of God's Love* characters on page 16 of this guide. Hold up the punch-out figures of Abby and Jamal one at a time and ask the children to tell you the name of each character *(Abby and Jamal)* as you show them each punch-out.

—What did Miss Diaz tell Jamal and Abby about Jesus? *(Jesus loves all of us.)*

Apply

Work on the children's leaflet activity.

- Have several children assist you in handing out the children's leaflet for chapter 2. Have all the children look at the cover to recall the story and then open their leaflet to the activity pages.
- Provide crayons or markers and invite them to color the hearts next to their favorite things. Call upon each of the children by name and have them share their favorite things with the group. This sharing will help the children come to know each other better.
- Be sure to write the name of each of the children and the date on the back of their work.

Connect with the child's life.

- Call attention to the back page of the children's leaflet and tell the children that this page is for their family. Ask the children what things they will tell their families that they like to do in religion class.
- Remind the children to take their leaflet home and to share the story on the For My Family Page and the activity or ask their parents to reread the story with them.

My Favorite Things

Color the hearts next to your favorite things.
Ask a friend to tell you about their favorite things.

Pray

- Gather the children at the prayer table.
- Introduce the prayer by saying, "Today we will thank Jesus for being our friend and for all of our friends."
- Quiet the children by having them repeat after you, "My head I bow. / My hands I fold. / Now I talk to God." *(Pause.)*
- Lead the children in prayer.

Teacher:	Thank you, Jesus, for being my friend.
Children:	Thank you, Jesus, for being my friend.
Teacher:	Thank you, Jesus, for all of my friends.
Children:	Thank you, Jesus, for all of my friends.
Teacher:	Together let us pray, "Amen."
All:	Amen.

Additional Activities

Use these activities as good ways for children to get to know each other, learn how to take turns and have some fun.

Build with blocks.

- Provide a variety of blocks in the Story Time Area in the room.
- Laminate the punch-out figures or cover them with clear contact paper, then tape them to blocks so they will stand.
- Hang the teaching poster near this area.
- Invite children to build structures for the "Stories of God's Love" children, such as a church, house or school.
- Talk to the children about making new friends and encourage them to work together as they build.

Play "Duck, Duck, Goose."

- Invite the children to sit in a circle on the floor. Select a child to walk around the outside of the circle, tapping each child gently on the shoulder saying, "duck."
- Whenever they choose, the child walking around will tap one child and say, "goose."
- The child tagged immediately gets up and chases the other around the outside of the circle. If the child being chased gets back to the other's spot before getting caught, the tagged child becomes the new person who walks around the circle choosing a duck or goose.

CHAPTER 3

Jesus Is the Good Shepherd

Background
for the Catechist

The Good Shepherd

When Jesus used the image of a good shepherd with the people of his time, they would certainly have understood what he was saying. They were quite familiar with the role of a shepherd.

A shepherd's entire life was centered around his flock. Every need of his sheep was both anticipated and met as the shepherd knew and cared for each sheep individually. A good shepherd kept his flock from harm and was willing to lay down his life for the safety of his sheep.

The sheep of a good shepherd, in turn, knew that they were protected from danger and cared for. The sheep of a good shepherd trusted the shepherd. When they heard the voice of their shepherd, they would respond to his voice and would only follow his voice.

The image of the good shepherd helps us understand the mystery of the great love and care that Christ has for his flock, the Church. When he describes himself as the Good Shepherd, Jesus invites us to respond to him with the deepest of trust.

For Reflection

When have I placed my trust in Jesus? What can I do this week to help the children develop a sense of trust in Jesus' love for them?

About the Children

Three- and young four-year-olds are beginning to develop the language and social skills needed to establish peer relationships and to include others in their play. In planning a cooperative learning environment, be sure to capitalize on the developmental strengths of this age group. Encourage peer conversations and interaction. Children this age also have wonderful imaginations and generally like to use objects symbolically. For example, a block of wood can become a truck, a ramp or a telephone. By providing age-appropriate materials you can give children the opportunity to use their imaginations in learning situations.

A Few Suggestions . . .

Building relationships is a new skill for children at these ages. By creating an atmosphere that encourages and provides opportunities for cooperation and interaction, you will be assisting the children in the development of good relationship-building skills. The activities and crafts in the Welcome Center and the activities throughout the lessons can help children practice the social skills of taking turns and talking to their peers. These skills are important for successful social growth.

More Background

For further reading and reflection see *Catechism of the Catholic Church §§ 753, 754; Compendium—Catechism of the Catholic Church § 148; United States Catholic Catechism for Adults* pages 258, 259.

Lesson Planner

Faith Focus

Jesus is the Good Shepherd who knows his sheep by name.

Bible Story

"I Am the Good Shepherd" (Based on John 10:3–5, 11, 14–15)

Enriching the Lesson

- RCL Benziger *Stories of God's Love* Music CD and companion Songbook, Song 2
- Visit our preschool Web site www.RCLBenzigerPreschool.com this week.

Chapter Objectives

After this week's lesson the children should be able to:

- recall the Bible story "I Am the Good Shepherd."
- discover that Jesus loves and cares for them.
- thank the people who love and care for them.

Materials Needed

In addition to the general supplies named on page 9 of this guide, you will need the following materials for teaching this lesson:

- copies of connect-the-dots activity master on page 154 of the guide, one for each of the children
- closed Bible with bookmark at John 10:3–5, 11, 14–15
- small stuffed sheep or plastic sheep

Prayer

Lord God, Father of all,
you sent your Son, Jesus,
as the Good Shepherd
who watches and cares for his sheep.
Be with me this week
as I teach the children about your great love.
Amen.

3 Jesus Is the Good Shepherd

Stories of God's Love
Ages 3 and 4

"I Am the Good Shepherd"

One day Jesus was talking with some people. He wanted them to know how much he loved them and that he cared about them. The people knew all about sheep. Many people had sheep and took care of them.

Jesus told the people, "I am the Good Shepherd. I know my sheep. My sheep know me. My sheep know that I take good care of them."

Jesus said to the people, "A good shepherd takes care of his sheep. The good shepherd knows his sheep by name. The sheep trust their shepherd. They come to him when he calls them."

Jesus then told the people what a good shepherd does. He said, "A good shepherd keeps his sheep safe."

Jesus then told the people something very important. He said, "Just as God my Father loves and cares for me, I love and care for the people my Father gave to me."

Jesus wants us to know today that he is our Good Shepherd. He loves and cares for us, his friends.

BASED ON JOHN 10:3–5, 11, 14–15

 Welcome

- Provide copies of the activity master found on page 154 of this guide, one for each of the children.
- Greet the children and direct them to the Welcome Center. Give each of the children an activity sheet, and invite the children to connect the dots to discover the animal.
- Walk among the children as they are working on the activity. As they finish connecting the dots, ask, "What kind of animal did you make?" *(A sheep)* Have all the children echo after you, "These animals are sheep."
- Tell the children that the Bible story today will be about sheep.

 Gather

- Play the theme song on the *Stories of God's Love* Music CD or the gathering song you have selected to use this year to signal the children that it is time for them to clean up and move to the Story Time Area.
- Tell the children that you will play a new song. Invite the children to listen to song 2, the song for unit 1 (chapters 3–6). If you are not using the *Stories of God's Love* Music CD, play another appropriate song. Play the song and demonstrate motions to accompany the lyrics. Repeat playing the song and demonstrating as needed.

 Teach

Introduce the Bible story.

- Show the children the teaching poster or the cover of the children's leaflet for chapter 3. Read aloud the title "Jesus Is the Good Shepherd." Repeat the word *shepherd* aloud and have the children echo it after you. Ask, "Who can tell me what a shepherd is?" Summarize by explaining to the children that a shepherd is someone who takes care of sheep. Invite the children to repeat the word *shepherd* after you.
- Ask the children to listen to the Bible story about Jesus and discover what he tells the people about himself.

Tell the Bible story.

Invite a child to come up and open the Bible to the place marked by the bookmark, John 10:3–5. Take the opened Bible and place the children's leaflet inside. Tell the children the name of the Bible story "I Am the Good Shepherd." Refer to the teaching poster or the cover of the children's leaflet as you read the Bible story on the Family Page to the children.

Recall the Bible story.

- Tell the children that you are going to ask them a question. Explain to them that they are to raise both of their hands if they know the answer to the question. Ask, "What kind of shepherd did Jesus say he was?" *(a good shepherd)* Give a stuffed or plastic sheep to one of the children who raised their hands. Invite the child holding the sheep to answer the question.

- Ask the child to pass the sheep to another child. Ask the child who is now holding the sheep, "What does a good shepherd do for the sheep?" *(Cares for them, keeps them safe. Accept other appropriate answers, such as, feeds them, gives them water to drink and so on not named in the Bible story.)*
- Point to the title on the teaching poster or cover of the leaflet and have the children echo after you, "Jesus Is the Good Shepherd." Conclude by telling the children that Jesus loves and cares for them.

Apply

Work on the children's leaflet activity.

- Have several children assist you in handing out the children's leaflet for chapter 3. Have all the children briefly look at the cover of the leaflet to recall the Bible story.
- Ask the children to open the leaflet to the activity pages. Call their attention to the pictures of the helpers they see on the pages. Talk with the children about how these people help care for them or other people.
- Have the children look at the pictures on the bottom of the page of the different tools that the helpers in the pictures use to help people. Invite the children to draw lines to match the tools to the helpers who use them.

Connect with the child's life.

- Ask the questions and congratulate the children for responding:
    - —Who loves and cares for you?
    - —What can you do to show your love for the people at home who love and care for you?
- Remind the children to take their leaflet home and to share the Bible story and activity with their family.

People Who Care for Us

Match each tool to the helper who uses it.
Say "Thank you" to someone who takes care of you.

Pray

- Gather the children at the prayer table.
- Introduce the prayer by saying, "Today we will thank God for all of the people who love and care for us. Tell the children that they will pray aloud, "Thank you, God" each time you name some of the people who love and care for them.
- Quiet the children by having them repeat after you, "My head I bow. / My hands I fold. / Now I talk to God." *(Pause.)*
- Lead the children in prayer.

Teacher:	For Jesus the Good Shepherd, thank you, God.
Children.	Thank you, God.
Teacher:	For *(invite the children to name the people who love and care for them. After each child names someone pray aloud,* "Thank you, God.")
Children:	Thank you, God.
Teacher:	Together let us pray, "Amen."
All:	Amen.

Additional Activities

Play "Follow the Shepherd."

Use this activity to reinforce the children's understanding of the Bible story "I Am the Good Shepherd."

- Briefly retell the Bible story. Emphasize that the shepherd knows his sheep by name, and the sheep recognize their shepherd and will follow only him.
- Invite the children to play a follow-the-leader type game. Have the children line up behind you and march around the room, chanting, "We follow our shepherd, our shepherd, our shepherd. We are following our shepherd, wherever he will lead."
- Next, tell the children to use the motions you are going to show them as they march and chant. Demonstrate these motions as you say the chant aloud, "We follow . . ." and have the children imitate you. You might move arms in a pumping motion, jump instead of march, or clap your hands as you march. Change your action several times, alerting the children each time you change.
- After the children are familiar with the words and motions invite one of the children to be the leader. Let the children take turns being the shepherd and leading the class in the activity.

Play with farm animals.

Use this activity to reinforce the concept of caring for others.

- Provide figures of farm animals, including several sheep, and figures of people, and display the teaching poster in the Story Time Area.
- Invite the children to use the people figures to pretend to care for the animals.

45

My Name Is Special

Background
for the Catechist

Called by Name

In the Old Testament, Isaiah the Prophet reminds us that God calls each of us by name and identifies us as his own. (See Isaiah 43:1). In the Bible story from chapter 3, John gives the account of Jesus describing himself, using the image of the Good Shepherd, who knows and calls each of his sheep by name. (See John 10:3–5, 11, 14–15.)

Our names carry our very identity. To be known "by name" means to be known individually and personally. To be known by name by God points to an intimacy with God the Father, God the Son and God the Holy Spirit who knows us, addresses (calls) us and loves us.

God created human beings in his own image and likeness. He created us to be sharers in his own life. In this is rooted our dignity. We are called to honor and respect others, seeing everyone as a child of God and a member of God's family. We are to treat each person with the dignity that is given them by God.

For Reflection

What does it mean to me that God knows and loves me by name, knows and loves me individually and personally? What can I do to help the children recognize that God knows each of them and loves each of them?

About the Children

People who work with three- and young four-year-olds are often amazed at how quickly they develop spoken language. They are also surprised by the misinterpretations that are common with young learners. For example, when saying something like, "Don't run," it can be common to see children at this age sometimes pick up speed. Oftentimes they hear the word *run* but do not process the word *don't*. It takes some time for children this age to fully connect with abstract words such as *don't, can't* and *mustn't*. Be patient with the children, repeat instructions, and model the action you are asking them to do.

A Few Suggestions . . .

One of the best techniques for communicating effectively with three- and four-year-olds is to use positive language. For example, saying "Walk" instead of "Don't run" is much more likely to get a positive response. It can also be helpful to suggest a replacement activity. For example, instead of saying, "Don't put your fingers in your mouth," it can be more effective to suggest, "Put your fingers in your lap." Using positive language will lead to clearer communication and a more pleasant learning environment.

More Background

For further reading and reflection see *Catechism of the Catholic Church* §§ 355–361, *Compendium—Catechism of the Catholic Church* § 66, *United States Catholic Catechism for Adults* pages 67–68, 71, 73–75, 310.

Lesson Planner

Faith Focus

God knows and loves each one of us by name.

Story

"Carlos and Grandpa Go to the Park"

Enriching the Lesson

- RCL Benziger *Stories of God's Love* Music CD and companion Songbook, Song 2
- Visit our preschool Web site www.RCLBenzigerPreschool.com this week.

Chapter Objectives

After this week's lesson the children should be able to:

- recall the story "Carlos and Grandpa Go to the Park."
- discover that their names are special.
- celebrate that we are special and our friends are special.

Materials Needed

In addition to the general supplies named on page 9 of this guide, you will need the following materials for teaching this lesson:

- chart paper with heading "Our Special Names"
- card or one-half sheet of paper with children's names, one for each of the children
- punch-outs of Carlos, one for each of the children

Prayer

God our Creator,
you know me and call me by name.
Help me reach out to others and
honor their dignity as your image.
Send the Holy Spirit of your love
to be with me as I teach the children
about your great and awesome love.
Amen.

Carlos and Grandpa Go to the Park

Carlos was very excited. "Mom, is it time yet?" he called out.

Mom answered, "Almost. Just watch from the front window."

Today was the day Grandpa was coming to take Carlos to the park. Carlos loved his grandpa very much. He knew Grandpa loved him too. They did something special every Saturday, just the two of them.

When Grandpa came to the door, Carlos ran to him. He jumped into his arms, and Grandpa swung him around.

"WHEE!" squealed Carlos. "Let's go, Grandpa. Let's go to the park right now!"

Grandpa said, "OK. Bye everyone. We're going to the park. See you later."

At the park Carlos took Grandpa's hand and led him to the swings. "Push me. Please, Grandpa?" he asked.

Grandpa laughed and said, "That is exactly what I used to say to my grandpa when I was a little boy."

Carlos looked up to Grandpa and asked, "What did he say back to you?"

"Let's see," Grandpa said, as he was trying to remember. "I think my grandpa said 'Carlos, I love you and I'll push you as long as you like.' "

Carlos' eyes got very big and he smiled with excitement. "Grandpa, your name is Carlos too? Just like my name!"

Grandpa put his gentle hand on Carlos' head. "I know," he said. "Your parents love me and wanted you to have the same name. It shows they love us both very much. Our names are very special."

"I'm glad we have the same name," whispered Carlos as he gave Grandpa a big hug. "Now, let's go swing!"

 Welcome

- Provide a chart with the heading "Our Special Names"; one-half sheets of paper, one for each of the children with their name printed on it; crayons or markers.
- Greet the children by name and direct them to the Welcome Center. Help each child find the card or paper with their name printed on it.
- Have the children use the crayons, markers and other materials to decorate their name card. Walk among the children as they are working. Address each child by name and encourage them to greet one another by name when they arrive for class, work together during class, play together and so on.
- Tell them that each of their names is special. Invite the children to tape or glue their decorated name card to the "Our Special Names" chart.

 Gather

- Play the gathering song to signal that it is time for the children to clean up and move to the Story Time Area.
- Lead the children in singing song 2 for unit 1 on the *Stories of God's Love* Music CD or another appropriate song.
- Call the children's attention to the chart they made and tell them that their names are special to their families, to you and to the other teachers, and to God.
- Explain to them that when they talk with God in prayer, they can begin by saying, "Dear God, this is *(name)*."

 Teach

Introduce the story.

- Show the children the teaching poster or the cover of the children's leaflet for chapter 4. Point to and read the title of the story "Carlos and Grandpa Go to the Park" to the children.
- Invite the children to listen to why Carlos' name was special to him.

Tell the story.

Tell the children the name of the story "Carlos and Grandpa Go to the Park." Refer to the illustration on the teaching poster or cover of the children's leaflet as you read the story to the children.

Recall the story.

- Hand out a punch-out of Carlos to each of the children. Tell the children to hold up their punch-out figure of Carlos if they know the answer to the questions that you will ask them. Ask these questions:
    - —Who came to visit Carlos? *(His grandpa)*
    - —What did Carlos and his grandpa do? *(They went to the park and played on the swings.)*

—Why was Carlos happy? *(Because Carlos has the same name as his grandpa)*

- Congratulate the children for remembering the story so well.

 Apply

Work on the children's leaflet activity.

- Ask several children to assist you in handing out the children's leaflet for chapter 4. Point to the title, say it aloud and invite the children to echo it after you.
- Have the children open their leaflet to the activity pages. Explain the directions for the activity and have the children decorate the banner while you help them print their names on the line.
- Conclude by telling the children that each of their names is special because each of them is special. Help the children recall the Bible story "Jesus Is the Good Shepherd" that you told them last time they came to religion class. If necessary, summarize the story to help the children recall it. Tell them that Jesus knows each of their names. He loves each of them.

Connect with the child's life.

- Have the children ask their parents why their name is so special.
- Remind the children to take their leaflet home and to share the story on the For My Family Page and the activity with their family. Tell the children to tell their parents the names of their new friends in religion class.

 Pray

- Gather the children at the prayer table.
- Introduce the prayer by telling the children that they will sing the prayer today. Have the children practice the prayer by singing it to the tune of "Where Is Thumbkin?"

   I am special, I am special. *(Point to self.)*
   Yes, I am, Yes, I am.
   I am very special, I am very special.
   God made me. God made me. *(Fold hands in prayer.)*

I Have a Special Name
My Name Is

Write your name. Decorate the banner.
Tell your name to a new friend.

- Have them pray silently, "Dear God, this is *(name of child)*." Lead the children in prayer.
- Conclude by praying together, "Thank you, God. Amen."

Additional Activities

Paint the letters of their names.

Use this activity to help the children begin to recognize the letters in their special name.

- Provide sponges cut in the shapes of the alphabet (these can be found at a teaching- or art-supply store), tubs or trays of washable tempera paint, pieces of art paper and a copy of each child's name.
- Assist the children in putting on paint smocks.
- Help the children select the sponge letters they will need to "paint" their names. Help the children who need assistance in recognizing the letters in their name.
- Invite the children to dip the letters, one at a time, in the tempera paint to make the letters of their name on a piece of paper.
- Walk among the children as they are painting their names. Address the children by their names and tell them that just as each of their names is special, they are special.

Create a classroom mural.

Use this activity to extend the activity in the children's leaflet.

- Provide crayons and markers, several small hand-held mirrors and a piece of paper long enough to make a mural. In advance, draw a picture of yourself with your name printed under it in colorful letters and write the heading "We Are Special. Our Names Are Special" across the top of the mural.
- Direct the children to the Art Center. Ask them to look at the picture that you have drawn of yourself on the mural. Give each of the children an outline of a boy or girl. Ask the children to look in the mirror. Help them identify their eye color, skin color and the color and length of their hair. Have them add these and other details, such as freckles, to the outline. Walk among the children and write their names next to their pictures.
- Hang the mural in the classroom or out in the hall near the entrance to the room for all to see.

Use foam letters to get to know the alphabet.

Use this activity to familiarize the children with the letters of the alphabet that make their names.

   Provide paper and glue and letters of the alphabet cut out of foam. Invite the children to construct their name or to just play with and get familiar with the alphabet.

49

The Good Shepherd Cares for His Sheep

CHAPTER 5

Background
for the Catechist

The Care of a Shepherd

The image of the good and caring shepherd is found in several places throughout the Gospels. An image was explored earlier in chapter 3. The image of the good shepherd in that chapter emphasized the intimacy with which the shepherd knew his sheep, both individually as well as collectively.

The Bible story in this chapter also uses the image of the good shepherd and points to the mystery of God's love and care for all, especially for the "lost"—those who turn away from his love. The image of the shepherd looking for and finding his lost sheep reveals the joy with which God rejoices when he welcomes the person who turns back toward and accepts God's love.

In Luke's Gospel Jesus uses the image of a good shepherd to counter the challenge and complaints from the Pharisees who were upset that Jesus was welcoming and dining with those they considered sinners (see Luke 15:4–7). Jesus admonished them that he was acting with the same care and compassion that God the Father shows to all.

For Reflection

In what ways do I know that I am loved and cared for by God? What can I do to help create a loving and welcoming community in my classroom this week?

About the Children

Play is an effective and powerful way for young children to learn. Play is the work of childhood, the primary method for children to practice new skills and learn about themselves, others and their world. By commenting, prompting and expanding on what the children are saying while they are at play, you help them as their language skills are enhanced and new vocabulary is learned.

A Few Suggestions . . .

Children not only want to play but they need the active-learning and child-focused activities associated with play. Setting up your lessons in a way that allows children to engage in play will lead them to being on task. Structured play in a classroom setting means providing opportunities for children to have fun with their peers while exploring the key concepts of the chapter. Play also means that children have the opportunity to be active, to use materials to build and create and to learn by acting out stories.

More Background

For further reading and reflection see *Catechism of the Catholic Church* §§ 753, 754, *Compendium—Catechism of the Catholic Church* § 148, *United States Catholic Catechism for Adults* pages 258, 259.

Lesson Planner

Faith Focus

The love of a good shepherd for each and every one of his sheep helps us come to know that God loves each and every one of us.

Bible Story

"The Good Shepherd Cares for His Sheep" (Based on Luke 15:4–7)

Enriching the Lesson

- RCL Benziger *Stories of God's Love* Music CD and companion Songbook, Song 2
- Visit our preschool Web site www.RCLBenzigerPreschool.com this week.

Chapter Objectives

After this week's lesson the children should be able to:

- recall the Bible story "The Good Shepherd Cares for His Sheep."
- discover that God loves and cares for everyone.
- share ways they can thank God for those who love and care for them.

Materials Needed

In addition to the general supplies named on page 9 of this guide, you will need the following materials for teaching this lesson:

- construction paper cut into bookmark size and stickers of heart shapes and sheep and other appropriate images
- closed Bible with bookmark placed at Luke 15:4–7

Prayer

Lord God,
when I turn away from you,
I know that you always
welcome me back.
Help me always welcome the children
and be an example of your great love
and care for them.
Amen.

5 The Good Shepherd Cares for His Sheep

Stories of God's Love
Ages 3 and 4

The Good Shepherd Cares for His Sheep

The last time we listened to a story about Jesus, Jesus told us that he is the Good Shepherd. A good shepherd knows each of his sheep by name. He loves and cares for his sheep. Jesus told the story to teach us how much God loves us.

One time Jesus told another story about how much a good shepherd loves and cares for his sheep. This is what Jesus told them.

Jesus said, "There was a Good Shepherd who had many sheep. One day one of the sheep wandered away from the shepherd and the rest of the sheep. The sheep got lost."

Jesus went on to tell the people, "The shepherd searched and searched. He kept looking everywhere for his lost sheep. He didn't stop until he found the sheep."

Jesus then told the people, "The shepherd was very happy when he found his lost sheep. The shepherd picked up the sheep and put it over his shoulders and carried it home. Seeing his neighbors and friends he called out, 'Look, I found my sheep. Be happy with me!' "

BASED ON LUKE 15:4–7

 Welcome

- Provide pieces of construction paper cut into bookmark size on which you have written "God Loves Me" on one side and the child's name and date on the other; and appropriate stickers, such as, shapes of hearts, of sheep and of other appropriate images.
- Greet the children and direct them to the Welcome Center. Give each child their bookmark. Tell them to use the stickers to decorate their bookmarks.
- Collect the finished bookmarks to give to the children at prayer time.

 Gather

- Play the gathering song to signal that it is time for the children to clean up and move to the Story Time Area.
- Lead the children in singing song 2 for unit 1 on the *Stories of God's Love* Music CD or another appropriate song.

 Teach

Introduce the Bible story.

- Use the teaching poster or the cover of the children's leaflet for chapter 3 to help the children recall the Bible story of Jesus the Good Shepherd that they heard in chapter 3. Remind the children that a good shepherd is one who takes care of sheep. Remind the children of some of the characteristics of a good shepherd, namely a good shepherd knows each one of his sheep, a good shepherd loves everyone of his sheep, a good shepherd protects his sheep.
- Show the children the teaching poster or the illustration on the cover of the children's leaflet for this chapter, chapter 5. Ask the children to listen to another Bible story to discover what a good shepherd does when his sheep get lost.

Tell the Bible story.

Invite a child to come up and open the Bible to the place marked by the bookmark, Luke 15:4–7. Take the opened Bible, place the children's leaflet inside. Tell the children the name of the Bible story "The Good Shepherd Cares for His Sheep." Refer to the teaching poster or the cover of the children's leaflet as you read the Bible story on the For My Family Page to the children.

Recall the Bible story.

Help the children recall the Bible story by leading them in singing the following song to the tune of "Mary Had a Little Lamb." Tell them to fill in the missing word when you stop singing.

The shepherd had many sheep, / many sheep,
many sheep. / The shepherd had many *(stop)*. /
He watched them day and night.
One little sheep went far away, far away, far away. / One
little sheep went far *(stop)*. / The little sheep was lost.

The shepherd went and looked for him, / looked for him, looked for him. / The shepherd went and *(stop)* for him. / He loved the little sheep.

When he found it he was glad, / he was glad, / he was glad. / When he found it, he was *(stop)*, / the sheep was finally home.

Apply

Work on the children's leaflet activity.

- Ask several children to assist you in handing out the children's leaflet for chapter 5. Have all the children briefly look at the picture on the cover of the leaflet to help them recall the Bible story.
- Ask the children to open the leaflet to the activity pages. Invite them to describe to you what they see. Explain that they are to help the shepherd find the lost sheep by tracing a path from the shepherd to the lost sheep.
- Walk among the children as they are working on the activity and assist those children who need help in tracing the path. Remind them that Jesus told us this story to tell us that God loves and cares for us just as the good shepherd in the Bible loves and cares for his sheep.

Connect with the child's life.

- Ask the question, "What could you do or say this week to thank the people who love and care for you?" Give examples, if necessary, to help the children respond. Congratulate the children for responding by using brief statements, such as, "That would be a wonderful way to thank your *(parents)*."
- Tell the children to take home their leaflet and share the Bible story on the For My Family Page and the activity with their families.

Pray

- Gather the children around the prayer table. Tell the children that in today's prayer they will repeat the words of the prayer after you.
- Call the children to a moment of silence. *(Pause.)* Lead the children in prayer.

Teacher: Thank you, God, for loving us.
Children: Thank you, God, for loving us.

Teacher: Thank you, God, for giving us people who love and care for us.
Children: Thank you, God, for giving us people who love and care for us.
Teacher: Thank you, God, for our families and teachers who love and care for us.
Children: Thank you, God, for our families and teachers who love and care for us.
Teacher: Together let us pray, "Amen."
All: Amen.

Additional Activities

Find the sheep.

Use this activity to help the children recall the story of the good shepherd and the lost sheep.

- Tape sheep made from the activity master on page 155 of this guide, one picture of a sheep for each of the children, in plain sight around the room and at a height that the children can reach them. In addition provide crayons, cotton balls and glue.
- Hold up and show one of the pictures of the sheep that you made for the activity to the children. Tell them that you have hidden a picture like the one you are holding for each of them to find around the room.
- Instruct the children that when you say "Go," they are to get up and walk slowly around the room until they each find one picture. Tell them to stand by the picture when they find it. When all the children have found a picture of one of the sheep and are standing by it, say, "You all are good shepherds. You found your sheep."
- Instruct the children to carefully take the picture down and bring it to the table. Tell them to use the crayons, cotton balls and glue to decorate their sheep. Display the decorated sheep around the classroom or have the children take them home.

Play a shepherd-and-sheep circle game.

Use this activity to reinforce the Bible story.

- Gather the children together and have them sit in a circle on the floor. Retell the Bible story.
- Play this game. Choose one child to be the lost sheep and have the rest of the children be shepherds. Have the shepherds cover their eyes and tell the lost sheep to hide in the room. Tell the shepherds that you will count to 10 and then say, "Go." When they hear the word "Go," they are to uncover their eyes. You will then choose one of the shepherds to find the lost sheep. When the shepherd finds the lost sheep, he or she is to bring the sheep back to the circle area. Repeat the playing of the game.

Finding the Lost Sheep

Draw a line from the good shepherd to the lost sheep.
Tell Jesus, "Thank you, Jesus. You are our Good Shepherd."

My Family Cares for Me

Background
for the Catechist

The Christian Family

In Isaiah 66:13 we read, "As a mother comforts her [child], / so I will comfort you." Through this beautiful picture of the love and care we can find in a family, God reveals the depths of his love for us.

God reveals that his very nature is love (see 1 John 4:8) and that he lives in a mystery of loving communion who is Father, Son and Holy Spirit. Created in God's image, we are reminded that love is at the heart of who we are and are called to be individually, as members of our family, as members of the Church and as members of the human community.

The Christian family is the living image of the Holy Trinity in the world. It points to God and nurtures the relationship of its members with God. It is in the relationship of the family that young children first begin to understand the love and care of God for them and for all people. Through the mutual love and respect that bind children and their parents, children discover God's love for them. This experience of love within their family becomes foundational to a child's growing in love for God.

For Reflection

What do I do to give witness to and to nurture the love of God with my family? What can I do to support the families of the children in their responsibility to nurture their children in faith and in their love for God?

About the Children

During these early years, children form attitudes about learning that will last a lifetime. Children who receive proper support and encouragement during these years will be creative, adventurous learners throughout their lives. Young children learn from everything they do. They are naturally curious and want to explore and discover, and may become easily excited about new classroom activities.

A Few Suggestions . . .

It is important to balance the need for children to experience independence with the need for safe supervision. Create a class-room environment where exploration creates excitement and success encourages the children to want to learn more. Talk with the children about classroom behaviors that will help them work together. Praise the children's efforts in being curious and creative while at the same time giving them clear parameters for expected behavior. This will create a positive and enjoyable learning environment that fosters independence.

More Background

For further reading and reflection see *Catechism of the Catholic Church* 218–221, 295, 2201–2203, 2205; *Compendium— Catechism of the Catholic Church* 42, 460; *United States Catholic Catechism for Adults* pages 51–53, 61, 103–104, 118–119, 375–380.

Lesson Planner

Faith Focus

My family loves and cares for me.

Story

"Music Across the Street"

Materials Needed

In addition to the general supplies named on page 9 of this guide, you will need the following materials for teaching this lesson:

- white paper plates, one for each of the children
- punch-outs of Kim, one for each of the children

Enriching the Lesson

- RCL Benziger *Stories of God's Love* Music CD and companion Songbook, Song 2
- Visit our preschool Web site www.RCLBenzigerPreschool.com this week.

Chapter Objectives

After this week's lesson the children should be able to:

- recall the story "Music Across the Street."
- discover that God gives them families that love and care for them.
- thank God for their families.

Prayer

Loving God,
Father, Son, and Holy Spirit,
you have created us
to live in a communion of love
with you and with one another.
Come, Holy Spirit,
strengthen us to live in that love.
Amen.

Music Across the Street

Kim was sitting on the front porch. The sun was shining and she was watching the children across the street. Her mom told her she was old enough to sit on the front porch all by herself for a few minutes. Kim felt like a big girl.

The boys and girls across the street were playing in the yard. It was fun to watch them jump around. They laughed as they chased one another. Kim knew that someday she would be old enough to go over and play with them. For now, she liked watching them.

Suddenly Kim heard loud music. One of the girls across the street brought music outside for the others to listen to. Kim loved music and wanted to get closer to hear it better. She jumped up and ran down the steps to go across the street.

Before she got there, Kim heard her mother's voice call out, "Kim, stop!"

Kim stopped and turned around. She saw her mother coming toward her. There was an unhappy look on her mom's face. Kim's mom came to her and took her hand. She walked Kim back to the porch where they sat down together.

"What, Mommy?" asked Kim. "I want to go hear the music."

"No, sweetie, you must never, never cross the street without a grown-up. I love you, and I want to keep you safe," her mother said.

Kim crawled up into her mother's lap and said, "I'm sorry, Mommy. I promise to never go across the street alone. Are you mad at me?"

Her mother held her tight and kissed her cheek. "I'm not mad at you. I just want to take good care of you because I love you with my whole heart. Now let's go in the house and listen to some of your favorite music."

Welcome

- Provide a white paper plate for each of the children on the back of which you have written the child's name and the date, and crayons and markers.
- Greet the children by name and direct them to the Welcome Center. Give each of the children their paper plate and ask them to draw a picture of their family on the side of the plate that does not have their name written on it.
- Walk among the children as they are working and remind them that they have been learning that God cares for them and loves them. Invite the children to tell you about who is in their family. Tell them that one way God shows his love for us is by giving us families who love us and care for us.

Gather

- Play the gathering song to signal that it is time for the children to clean up and move to the Story Time Area. Have the children bring the family plates they created to the Story Time Area. Invite the children to show and tell about their family plates. Collect the plates for use during the closing prayer.
- Lead the children in singing song 2 for unit 1 on the *Stories of God's Love* Music CD, or another appropriate song if you are not using the *Stories of God's Love* Music CD.

Teach

Introduce the story.

- Remind the children of the Bible story "The Good Shepherd Cares for His Sheep." Show them the teaching poster or the illustration on the cover of the children's leaflet for chapter 5 to help them recall the Bible story.
- Show the children the teaching poster or the cover of the children's leaflet for chapter 6 and read the title "My Family Cares for Me" to the children. Tell the children that today you will tell them a story about Kim. Invite the children to listen to discover how Kim's mom takes care of and shows her love for Kim.

Tell the story.

Tell the children the name of the story "Music Across the Street." Refer to the teaching poster or the cover of the leaflet for chapter 6 as you read the story to the children.

Recall the story.

- Hand out the punch-outs of Kim to each of the children. Tell the children that you are going to ask them three questions about the story. If they know the answer to a question, they are to hold up their punch-out of Kim. Tell them that you will call on someone to give the answer. Then after you receive the correct answer, you will hold up your punch-out of Kim and everyone is to say the answer out loud together. Briefly summarize the story:

Kim was sitting on the porch outside her home.
She saw children playing in the yard across the street.
One of the children brought music outside for the children to listen to.

- Ask:
  —When Kim heard the music, did she try to cross the street? *(Yes)*
  —Did Kim's mom watch her cross the street? *(No)* After the children say no, remind them what Kim's mom did.
  —Did Kim's mom bring Kim back to the porch because she loves Kim and wanted to keep Kim safe? *(Yes)*

 Apply

Work on the children's leaflet activity.

- Ask several children to assist you in handing out the children's leaflet for chapter 6. Have all the children briefly look at the picture on the cover of the leaflet to help them recall the story.
- Ask the children to open the leaflet to the activity pages. Invite them to tell you what they see the people doing. Tell the children to put their finger on the illustration of the mother and the baby. Ask, "What is missing in this picture?" *(bottle)* Instruct the children to take a marker and draw a line from the bottle to the picture of the mother and baby.
- Ask the children to put their finger on the next picture and repeat the process until all the matches have been made.
- Ask, "How are the people in the pictures showing their love?"
- Conclude by saying, "People show their love by caring for each other and the things they have."

Connect with the child's life.

- Ask the children to think of one way their families take care of them. Tell and encourage the children to say thank you to their families for taking care of them.
- Remind the children to take their leaflets home and to share the story on the For My Family Page and the activity with their family.

We Care for Each Other

Match the small pictures with the big pictures.
Tell how the people are showing their love.

 Pray

- Gather the children around the prayer table. Give each of the children the family plate they made, saying, "(Name), God loves you and gave you your family." Tell the children that they will pray aloud the words "Thank you, God, for my family" after you during the prayer.
- Lead the children in prayer.

Teacher:	My family loves me. Thank you, God, for my family.
Children:	My family loves me. Thank you, God, for my family.
Teacher:	My family takes care of me. Thank you, God, for my family.
Children:	My family takes care of me. Thank you, God, for my family.
Teacher:	Together let us pray, "Amen."
All:	Amen.

Additional Activities

Make a musical instrument.

Use this activity to reinforce the children's ability to recall the story "Music Across the Street."

- Provide two paper plates for each of the children, large paper clips and masking tape to seal the edges of the paper plates.
- Show the children the materials and tell them that they are going to make a musical instrument. Invite the children to decorate the bottom of the paper plates with markers or crayons.
- Assist the children in placing the plates with eating sides together and taping around the edges leaving a small opening not taped. Have the children take a small handful of paper clips and put them inside the opening. Finish taping the plates together securely so the paper clips do not come out when the children play their shakers.
- Lead the children in a song, letting them use their shakers to keep time with the music. Tell the children to take their instruments home and share their music with family members.

Paint to music.

Use this activity to encourage the children to thank someone in their family for caring for them.

- Provide 9-inch by 12-inch sheets of construction paper, small cups of washable paint and cotton swabs for brushes. Play the *Stories of God's Love* Music CD or other appropriate music as the children work.
- Invite the children to paint a picture to give to a family member as a way of thanking them for caring for them.
- Have the children share their paintings with each other.

CHAPTER 7

God Made the World

Background
for the Catechist

The Mystery of Creation

The Holy Spirit blesses us with the gift of "Wonder and Awe." This Gift of the Holy Spirit enables us to come to know the mystery of God present in our lives. One way we discover the mystery of God and his loving presence in our lives is through creation.

Creation is a manifestation of the goodness, beauty, love and power of God. While God truly transcends his creation, he is truly present to it. Because God is the Creator of all that is "seen and unseen," creation gives witness to his almighty love and goodness.

The Holy Spirit graces us with the Gift of Wonder and Awe. He gives us the power to discover in the beauty and goodness and order of the world the mystery of his presence to us. He invites us to come to know him and his love for us.

For Reflection

What parts of creation evoke in me a sense of the mystery of God's love? What can I do this week to help the children discover that creation is a gift of God given to us out of his love?

About the Children

Young children are filled with wonder and awe at the beauty and splendor of creation that surrounds them. This wonderful gift and ability is so natural that they often can be seen to be absorbed by even the seemingly simple experience of staring at a flower or watching a ladybug. Young children, who have not yet developed a sense of time, seem to live in the moment, overwhelmed by new sights and new experiences. Concepts of time, such as today, tomorrow and yesterday, or minute, hour, day and week, elude them.

A Few Suggestions . . .

Establish and keep a regular routine within your classroom. This will provide the children with a structure that enables them to predict events and activities. Post a daily schedule with pictures to remind the children of the plans for the lesson. Letting them know when a transition is coming can help them prepare and move more easily onto something new. Divide transitions into smaller steps. For example, use a regular signal, as *Stories of God's Love* does, to gather the children for story time. Some children will need longer or shorter transition times, so pay attention to each of their needs.

More Background

For further reading and reflection see *Catechism of the Catholic Church* §§ 279–281, 295–299, 337–349; *Compendium— Catechism of the Catholic Church* §§ 51–54; *United States Catholic Catechism for Adults* pages 53–56.

Lesson Planner

Faith Focus

God created the world. God's creation is good.

Bible Story

"God Made All Things Good" (Based on Genesis 1:1–25)

Enriching the Lesson

- RCL Benziger *Stories of God's Love* Music CD and companion Songbook, Song 3
- Visit our preschool Web site www.RCLBenzigerPreschool.com this week.

Chapter Objectives

After this week's lesson the children should be able to:

- recall the Bible story, "God Made All Things Good."
- discover that God made the world good.
- share that all God made is good.

Materials Needed

In addition to the general supplies named on page 9 of this guide, you will need the following materials for teaching this lesson:

- pictures of nature items in magazines or picture books, such as grass, flowers, trees, plants, animals, mountains, lakes and so on

Prayer

Lord, God, Creator of all
that is, seen and unseen,
may I never take for granted
your wonderful gift of creation.
Help me discover the presence of your love
in all you created.
Amen.

7 God Made the World

Stories of God's Love
Ages 3 and 4

God Made All Things Good

God made the sun and the moon,
The stars glimmering bright.
God looked at all he did and said,
"It is good."

God made the sea and the sky,
Full of fish and birds.
God looked at all he did and said,
"It is good."

God made the soil and the rock,
Plants and land animals of all kinds.
God looked at all he did and said,
"It is good."

BASED ON GENESIS 1:1–25

 ## Welcome

- Provide a variety of pictures of nature items, such as leaves, grass, flowers, seeds and trees. Picture books with these items could also be used.
- Greet the children by name and direct them to the Welcome Center. Show them the pictures of nature and give them time to look at and enjoy the pictures.
- Walk among the children as they are enjoying the pictures. Talk with them about which of the pictures are their favorites and have them tell you why they are their favorites.
- Pick up your favorite picture of creation, show it to the children and tell them why that part of creation is your favorite.

 ## Gather

- Play the gathering song to signal that it is time for the children to clean up and move to the Story Time Area.
- Tell the children that you will now play a new song that you will teach them. Play and teach the children song 3 for unit 2 on the *Stories of God's Love* Music CD. Or play another appropriate song about creation that you will teach the children and sing it with them during unit 2 (chapters 7, 8, 9 and 10) if you are not using the *Stories of God's Love* Music CD.

 ## Teach

Introduce the Bible story.

Show the children the illustration on the teaching poster or the cover of the children's leaflet for chapter 7. Recall for them the pictures that they looked at in the Welcome Center. Ask, "Who would like to hear a Bible story that tells us where all these wonderful things come from?" Tell the children to listen to learn who made all these things and gave them to us.

Tell the Bible story.

Invite a child to come up and open the Bible to the place marked by the bookmark, Genesis 1. Take the opened Bible and place the children's leaflet inside. Tell the children the name of the Bible story. Refer to the teaching poster or cover of the children's leaflet as you read the Bible story on the For My Family Page to the children. Pause each time you read the line "It is good" and have the children echo it after you.

Recall the Bible story.

- Teach the children this song retelling of the story of creation to help them recall it. Lead the children in singing it to a simple rhythm:
  Who made the sun and moon?
  God made the sun and moon!

Who made the earth and sky?
> God made the earth and sky!

Who made the lakes and sea?
> God made the lakes and sea!

Who made the fish that swim and birds that fly?
> God made the fish that swim and birds that fly!

Who made all the animals that walk on the land?
> God made all the animals that walk on the land!

Who made all that we can see and hear?
> God made all that we can see and hear!

- Conclude by asking the children to answer this question aloud together, "Who made the world and everything in it?" *(God)* Congratulate the children for their answers and say, "Yes, and God made everything good."

Apply

Work on the children's leaflet activity.

- Have several children assist you in handing out the children's leaflet for chapter 7. Have all the children briefly look at the cover of the leaflet. Then ask the children to open the leaflet and look at the activity pages.
- Call the children's attention to the illustrations and have them complete the pictures by connecting the dots.
- Walk among the children as they are working on the activity and assist the children who need help. Remind the children that God made and gave us all the wonderful things in the world. Everything God made is good.
- They can color the illustrations as time permits or complete the activity at home.

Connect with the child's life.

- Ask the children to name some of the things in nature, such as trees, the sky, flowers and birds that they see or hear on the way to religion class or at other times when they go on a walk with their family. Encourage them to tell their parents the things that they see or hear on the way home from religion class that God has made.
- Remind the children to take their leaflet home and share the Bible story and the activity with their families.

God Made Everything Good

Connect the dots. Tell what you see.
Thank God for our wonderful world.

 Pray

- Gather the children at the prayer table. Remind them that God has given us a beautiful world. Explain that in today's prayer you will thank God for all the wonderful things he has given us.
- Tell the children that they will pray the words "Thank you, God" and make the motions of the musical instrument you name.
- Quiet the children by having them pray silently after you, "My head I bow. / My hands I fold. / Now I talk to God." *(Pause.)* Lead them in prayer. Begin with the Sign of the Cross.

Teacher:	Let us thank God for the world and all the wonderful things he made. Thank you, God.
Children:	Thank you, God.
Teacher:	We thank God with the music of a drum. *(Make sound and motions.)*
Children:	*Repeat words, sound and motions.*
Teacher:	*Continue using other instruments. Conclude by saying,* "Together let us pray, "Amen."
All:	Amen.

Additional Activity

Use the sense of touch.

Use this activity to have the children use their sense of touch.

- Provide plastic sandwich bags that can be tightly sealed, one bag for each of the children, baby oil, food coloring, water and masking tape. Also provide a plastic sandwich bag already containing ½ cup of baby oil, ½ cup of water and a few drops of food coloring. Seal the opening and reinforce it with the masking tape.
- Show the children the squishy bag you have made. Lay the bag flat on the table and show the children how to move the oil and water around with your finger.
- Talk about all the different things in God's creation that we can experience with our senses. Talk about how some things are hard, some soft and some even squishy (children will enjoy using this fun word).
- Tell the children that they will now make their own squishy bag. Give each of them a plastic sandwich bag and assist them, one at a time, in pouring the baby oil and water and food coloring into their bag. Seal the bag and reinforce it with the masking tape. Write the child's name on the outside of the bag with a permanent marker.
- As you work with each child, invite the other children to play with the squishy bags you made before class.

CHAPTER 8

I Help Take Care of the World

Background
for the Catechist

Stewards of Creation

In the Book of Genesis God clearly gives humankind "dominion" over creation. We read that God said, "Let them have dominion over the fish of the sea, the birds of the air, and the cattle, and over all the wild animals and all the creatures that crawl on the ground" (see Genesis 1:26). What is the nature of this "dominion"?

In giving us "dominion" over his creation, God does not relinquish his ownership of creation. God does not abandon his "household," which is the root meaning of the word *dominion*. What God has done and continues to do is to give humankind the responsibility of being stewards of creation.

As we look at hunger and poverty in the world, global warming, air pollution and the selfish misuse and abuse of natural resources we can come to an understanding of the seriousness of this responsibility. Creation is ours to use as God intended. We are to use it for the glory of God and the goodness of all people. We are to manage wisely and generously what truly belongs to God in whose household, or *domus,* we live.

For Reflection

What do I do to care for creation? How well do my choices give glory to God? What can I do this week to nurture in the children both the attitude and behaviors of a good steward of creation?

About the Children

Three- and young four-year-olds generally want to please adults. They also have a need to be able to do things for themselves. If given the opportunity and time, they can pour their own drinks, use a spoon and fork and dress and undress themselves. They take pride in washing their own hands. With direction they learn to pick up after themselves, place trash in proper containers and turn off water faucets. All these actions help form the foundation of behaviors that enable the children to care for creation.

A Few Suggestions . . .

Teachers can support young children best by focusing on their strengths. By giving children enough time to do those things that they do well, teachers can capitalize on positive feelings and minimize frustration. Children this age also benefit from extended amounts of time for informal play. Time spent in play should be viewed as valuable learning time where children can practice new skills. Taking care of God's creation can be an excellent source of productive play. Provide materials that the children can use to develop and practice their skills to care for God's world.

More Background

For further reading and reflection see *Catechism of the Catholic Church* §§ 373, 2402 and 2415–2418; *Compendium—Catechism of the Catholic Church* §§ 503, 506 and 507; *United States Catholic Catechism for Adults* pages 450–457.

Lesson Planner

Faith Focus

We show our love for God when we take care of the world.

Story

"The Perfect Beach"

Enriching the Lesson

- RCL Benziger *Stories of God's Love* Music CD and companion Songbook, Song 3
- Visit our preschool Web site www.RCLBenzigerPreschool.com this week.

Chapter Objectives

After this week's lesson the children should be able to:

- recall the story "The Perfect Beach."
- discover ways to care for God's world.
- thank God for the beautiful ocean and all that he has given us.

Materials Needed

In addition to the general supplies named on page 9 of this guide, you will need the following materials for teaching this lesson:

- pictures of parts of creation we care for
- large blue circle cut out from 12-inch by 18-inch sheet of blue construction paper
- punch-out figure of Jamal, one for each of the children who will play Jamal; large beach towel; toy camera; bucket; paper cups and trash container

Prayer

Lord God,
Creator of all that is,
seen and unseen.
Strengthen my hands and my will
to wisely use
and generously share what,
first and above all, belongs to you.
Amen.

The Perfect Beach

Jamal ran onto the sandy beach. He loved the way it felt warm under his feet. "Come on, Mom and Dad. Let's start digging in the sand," he called.

They put their towels on the sand, unpacked Jamal's toys, and sat down to watch and listen to the ocean. It was blue and had large waves. They could hear the water as it hit the edge of the beach.

Jamal also saw children playing in the sand. They had bright yellow shovels and buckets. Jamal could hear them laughing.

Dad asked him, "Do you want to go get into the water? Let's go see what the water feels like. Then we'll play in the sand."

Jamal jumped up and down and said, "Let's go, Dad."

Jamal had so much fun running along the edge of the water with his dad. Jamal giggled and Mom took pictures. Mom brought them their buckets so they could build something in the sand. She also brought them some paper cups to help scoop sand.

After a little while, Jamal and his dad and mom had built a beautiful sand castle. Jamal stood back and looked at it. He thought it was the best one ever.

When Dad said it was time to pack up and go, Jamal grabbed the bucket and started walking back to the blanket with Mom. Dad called out, "Wait. Aren't we forgetting something?"

Jamal looked around and saw his dad pointing to the paper cups on the sand. Dad said, "Jamal, we can't leave the cups here. We need to clean up for the next visitors. God made this beautiful place for everyone. He wants us to take good care of it." Then Dad added, "Help me pick up the cups and put them in the trash container."

Jamal smiled at his dad and he and Mom helped Dad pick up the paper cups and put them in the trash. Jamal wanted the beach to be just perfect.

64

Welcome

- Provide pictures of animals and things we take care of, a circle shape cut from a large piece of blue construction paper to represent the earth, and glue or paste.
- Welcome the children and direct them to the Welcome Center. Talk with the children about what God has created. Say the word *creation* aloud and have the children echo the word *creation* with you. Tell the children that we use the word *creation* to name all that God has made.
- Show the children the earth shape made from the construction paper and the pictures. Tell the children that the blue paper circle stands for the earth. Invite the children to each choose a picture and glue or paste them on the earth shape.
- Walk among the children as they are working and remind them that God made the world and everything God made is good. Display the teaching poster or cover of the children's leaflet for chapter 7, if possible, to help them recall the Bible story.

Gather

- Play the gathering song you have chosen to signal that it is time for the children to clean up and move to the Story Time Area. Bring the earth poster the children have created to the Story Time Area and display it there.
- Lead the children in singing song 3 for unit 2 on the *Stories of God's Love* Music CD. Or lead the children in singing another appropriate song if you are not using the *Stories of God's Love* Music CD.

Teach

Introduce the story.

- Remind the children that last week they listened to a Bible story about creation. Show them the earth shape that they made in the Welcome Center and say, "God made and gave us all these wonderful things. God also wants us to take care of these things. God wants us to care for his creation."
- Show the children the teaching poster or the cover of the children's leaflet for this chapter and say, "Let us listen to a story about Jamal and find out what he and his mom and dad did to take care of creation."

Tell the story.

Tell the children the name of today's story "The Perfect Beach." Refer to the teaching poster or the cover of the children's leaflet for chapter 8 as you read the story to the children.

Recall the story.

- Provide the punch-out figure of Jamal, a towel, a toy camera, bucket, paper cups and a trash container.
- Help the children recall details of today's story by having the children dramatize the story with you.

- Invite the children to act out the story. Choose children to play Jamal, Mom and Dad. Hand out the punch-out figure of Jamal to the child who will be Jamal. Tell the children that you will say the words and that they will do the actions of the story.
- Lead the children in acting out the story. Conclude by telling the children, "Jamal and his mom and dad enjoyed the beach. But they made sure that they cleaned up. They took care of God's creation."

 ## Apply

Work on the children's leaflet activity.

- Ask several children to assist you in handing out the children's leaflet for chapter 8. Have all the children briefly look at the cover of the leaflet to recall today's story.
- Tell the children to open the leaflet and to look at the activity. Have the children tell you what they see at the beach.
- Explain the directions for the activity. Ask the children to draw a circle around the pictures of the things on the beach that do not belong on the beach and that they would put in the trash container.
- Walk among the children as they are circling the items. Remind them that God made the water and the beach. Tell them that when we pick up the items they circled and put them in the trash container we are taking care of God's creation.

Connect with the child's life.

- Ask the children this question, "What is one way you can help your family take care of God's creation this week?" Congratulate the children for their responses with brief statements, such as, "That would be a great way to take care of God's creation."
- Remind the children to take their leaflets home and share the story on the For My Family Page and the activity with their family.

 ## Pray

- Gather the children at the prayer table. Call them to a moment of silence and remind them that prayer time is the time when we talk to God. (Pause.)

Keep the Beach Clean

Take care of the beach.
Find and circle the trash.

- Lead the children in prayer. Have them echo the verses after you. Begin with the Sign of the Cross.

Teacher: God made the water blue.
Thank you, God, for water.
Children: Thank you, God, for water.
Teacher: *Add other parts of creation and have the children respond,*
Children: Thank you, God, for *(name part of creation.)*
Teacher: God, you gave us all these wonderful things. Help us take care of your world every day. Together let us pray, "Amen."
All: Amen.

Additional Activities

Play with God's seaside creation.
Use this activity to help the children discover the wonder of God's creation through the use of their sense of touch.

- Create a beach playscape in the pretend play area of your classroom, using items of a variety of textures. Provide buckets and shovels, a large beach towel, a beach ball, a tub of sand and stickers of sea creatures.
- Direct the children to the pretend play area. Show them the items and invite them to pretend that they are at the beach with their families. Invite them to play with the items.
- Talk with the children as they are playing about different ways the items feel. Name the different textures for the children, namely, rough, smooth, soft and hard.

Decorate a recycling container.
Use this activity to help the children develop the habit of caring for God's creation by learning to recycle paper and other items.

- Provide several small waste-collection containers that the children will decorate.
- Direct the children to the Art Center. Tell the children that there are many things that they use in class that we throw away that can be used again. Tell them that paper is one of those things.
- Show the children the containers. Tell them that they will decorate the containers and that the class will put the papers we throw away in these special containers.
- Have the children work in groups of two or three children to decorate the containers. Walk among the children as they are decorating the containers and tell them that by putting the paper in these special containers, they are helping to take care of God's creation.

CHAPTER 9

God Made People

Background
for the Catechist

In the Image of God . . .

The psalmist in reflecting on his dignity praises God, saying, "You formed my inmost being; / you knit me in my mother's womb. / I praise you, so wonderfully you made me; / wonderful are your works!" (Psalm 139:13–14).

Among all God's creatures, including the angels, the human person stands in a unique relationship with God. God created people to share in his love. God, for reasons beyond human comprehension, chose to create us in his divine image and likeness. In so doing he created us to share in the very life of God and invites us to live in communion with him, both now and forever.

Humankind's unique relationship with God establishes the sacredness and dignity of every human life. Such sanctity and dignity is at the heart and foundation of our identity. As we come to realize our unique relationship with God and the love of the Father for us, we will learn to love and respect ourselves and others with the love and respect every human person deserves.

For Reflection

What do I regularly say and do to show that I respect and reverence myself and others as images of God? What can I concretely do this week to help the children grow in their awareness that they are loved by God in a very special way?

About the Children

It was not so long ago that the children in your room were very possessive toddlers who were entranced by two magic words, "Mine" and "No." Now that the children have developed a better understanding of who they are and what is theirs, they are beginning to engage with some hesitation in activities that require cooperation and sharing. When faced with such activities, they need to use skills (cooperation and sharing) that are often beyond where they are developmentally and cognitively. They may have difficulty in considering the perspectives of others. This limitation should not be viewed as a lack of respect for others. It is simply where they are developmentally.

A Few Suggestions . . .

You can help the children successfully engage in activities and begin to learn social skills that will help them to respect the other children. Carefully consider and plan cooperative activities. Anticipate the children's responses to them. For example, have a plan for the sharing of toys. Use a timer that will signal that it is time for the children to take turns with other children. Your patient and positive guidance will go a long way toward helping the children develop these social skills.

More Background

For further reading and reflection see *Catechism of the Catholic Church* §§ 355–361 and 2415–2418, *Compendium—Catechism of the Catholic Church* §§ 66, *United States Catholic Catechism for Adults* pages 422 and 423.

Lesson Planner

Faith Focus

God created people to share in his love. We are special.

Bible Story

"God Made People Special" (Based on Genesis 1: 6-27)

Materials Needed

In addition to the general supplies named on page 9 of this guide, you will need the following materials for teaching this lesson:

- piece of white cloth material large enough to cover prayer table
- washable paint, shallow trays, water and paper towels
- closed Bible with bookmark placed at Genesis 1
- several handheld mirrors

Enriching the Lesson

- RCL Benziger *Stories of God's Love* Music CD and companion Songbook, Song 3
- Visit our preschool Web site www.RCLBenzigerPreschool.com this week.

Chapter Objectives

After this week's lesson the children should be able to:

- recall the Bible story "God Made People Special."
- discover that God made each of them special.
- thank God for making all people special.

Prayer

God our Creator,
we are wonderfully made
in your image and likeness.
May my words and actions
show the children
your love for each one of them.
Amen.

9 God Made People

Stories of God's Love
Ages 3 and 4

God Made People Special

God made the sun and the moon,
The stars glimmering bright.
God looked at all he did and said,
"It is good."

God made the sea and the sky,
Full of fish and birds.
God looked at all he did and said,
"It is good."

God made the soil and the rock,
Plants and land animals of all kinds.
God looked at all he did and said,
"It is good."

God then made people,
Special everyone.
God looked at what he did and said,
"It is very good."

BASED ON GENESIS 1:6–27

Welcome

- Provide a piece of white cloth large enough to make a cover for the prayer table, several shallow pans of washable tempera paint, paint brushes (one for each paint color), water and paper towels and a permanent marker or laundry marker.
- Greet the children by name and direct them to the Welcome Center. Tell them that each and every one of them is special.
- Help the children identify the different physical characteristics of their classmates, such as eye color, hair color and height. Point out that all these things tell others we are special. Then show your palm to the children and explain to them that everyone has a different handprint. Tell them that each of their handprints is so special that no one else has a handprint exactly like theirs.
- Show the children the shallow pans of paint and cloth and explain the activity. Tell them that they will decorate the cloth with their handprints to make a unique covering for the prayer table.
- Ask the children, one at a time, to choose a paint color. Take a paint brush and paint a thin layer of paint onto one of each child's hands. Let each child make several prints on the cloth. Write the children's names on the cloth near one of their handprints, using a laundry marker or permanent marker pen.
- Talk with the children as they are working. Tell them that each one of them is very special to God.

Gather

- Play the gathering song to signal that it is time for the children to clean up and move to the Story Time Area.
- Lead the children in singing song 3 for unit 2 on the *Stories of God's Love* Music CD. Or lead the children in singing the song that you have selected for unit 2 if you are not using the *Stories of God's Love* Music CD.

Teach

Introduce the Bible story.

- Recall with the children that they have been learning about God's creation. Repeat the word *creation* and have the children echo it after you. Remind them that we use the word *creation* to name all that God has made.
- Ask the children to name some of the things God created. Then show the children the teaching poster or the cover of the children's leaflet for chapter 9. Tell them that today you will tell them about the most special part of all God's creation. Invite the children to listen to discover what God has made that is so special.

Tell the Bible story.

Invite a child to come up and open the Bible to the place marked by the bookmark, Genesis 1. Take the opened Bible, place the children's leaflet inside. Refer to the teaching poster or cover of the children's leaflet as you read the Bible story on the For My Family Page to the children.

Recall the Bible story.

■ Help the children recall the Bible story by teaching and singing with them the following song, sung to the tune of "Mary Had a Little Lamb." Use these motions during the singing of the song: Point to the children and have the children point to you when saying the word *you* and point to yourself and have the children point to themselves when saying the word *me.* Have everyone hug themselves when they sing the line "He loves us very much."

> God made you *(point)* and God made me *(point).*
> You *(point)* and me *(point),* you *(point)* and me *(point)*
> God made you *(point)* and God made me *(point).*
> He loves us very much *(hug).*

■ Sing the song several times.

 ## Apply

Work on the children's leaflet activity.

■ Note: This activity will build on the activity the children did in the Welcome Center.
■ Provide several handheld mirrors and markers.
■ Ask several children to help you in handing out the children's leaflet for chapter 9. Have the children briefly look at the picture on the cover of the leaflet to help them recall the story. Read the title on the cover, "God Made People," out loud to the children.
■ Ask the children to open the leaflet to the activity pages and call their attention to the outline of the child (which is on the left page) and explain the activity. Help the children look in a handheld mirror and color their hair and eyes and skin to match the colors of their own hair and eyes and skin that they see in the mirror.
■ Tell the children, as they are working on their pictures, that God made us all special. Ask them to take their pictures home and ask their parents to help them trace and color the letters to discover the special message. *(God Made Me Special.)*

Connect with the child's life.

■ Tell the children to ask their parents to show them pictures of themselves as babies.
■ Remind the children to take home their leaflet and share the Bible story on the For My Family Page and the activity with their family.

 ## Pray

■ Invite the children to help you lay the decorated cloth they created at the beginning of class on the prayer table if it has dried. If it has not completely dried, place the cloth on the prayer table yourself.
■ Gather the children around the prayer table. Call the children to a moment of silence. *(Pause.)*
■ Lead the children in prayer. Begin with the Sign of the Cross.

Teacher:	For all the things you made,
Children:	we thank you, God.
Teacher:	For making *(name each child)* special,
Children:	we thank you, God
Teacher:	Together let us pray, "Amen."
All:	Amen.

Additional Activity

Make a "My Special People" book.

Use this activity to help the children appreciate that God made everyone special.

■ Provide a small booklet for each of the children made from a 9-inch by 12-inch piece of construction paper folded in half to serve as the cover, a piece of unlined paper folded in half for the pages and crayons or washable markers. Write the title "My Special People" on the front cover, using a marker.
■ Give each child a booklet and explain the activity. Ask the children to name four people who are special to them that they want to include in their booklets, for example, Mom, Dad, Nana, Pop Pop and so on. Note: The children may not name the same people so do not write these names in advance.
■ Write the names that each child identifies in their booklet, one name at the bottom (or top) of each page. Ask the children to use the crayons or washable markers to draw a picture of the person whose name you wrote on each page of their booklet. Be sure the variety of colors of the crayons and markers reflect hair colors and skin colors.
■ Talk with the children as they are drawing. Tell them that the people they are drawing are special to God just as they are. God loves them very much.
■ Continue as time allows and, if necessary, have the children take their booklets home and ask their parents to help them complete the project.

CHAPTER 10

I Take Care of Myself

Background
for the Catechist

Respect for Every Human Life

Life is a true gift. Our life—our spiritual and physical lives—is a gift from God. In the Book of Job we read, "In [God's] hand is the soul of every living thing, / and the life breath of all mankind" (Job 12:10). Created in the image and likeness of God, the human person is not something, but someone.

We have the responsibility to take care of our spiritual and physical well-being. Our bodies are temples of the Holy Spirit, temples of the living God. (See 1 Corinthians 6:19 and 2 Corinthians 6:16.) When we care for ourselves we give praise and thanks to God for the gift of life.

We also have the responsibility to respect the spiritual and physical lives of others. We are to respect all human life, born and unborn. We are to work to create conditions that promote the well-being of all who live within our society.

For Reflection

What do I do to express my gratitude for the gift of life? What do I do to care for both my physical and my spiritual health? What can I do this week to help the children learn to care for their well-being, both spiritually and physically?

About the Children

Many young children have very distinct tastes in regards to food. Getting them to try new things can be challenging. It is important to remember that solid food is still relatively new to young children. Taste buds are still developing and the connections to the sensory center of the brain are just beginning to form. Just as young children tend to be more comfortable with a consistent daily routine, many may decide they only want to eat a few familiar foods. The best thing to do is to provide a few healthful options at snack time.

A Few Suggestions . . .

As you are choosing healthful foods for class, you need to make sure that you carefully ask the parents about whether their children have food allergies. In selecting snacks, also choose foods that do not present a choking hazard. For example, while grapes are healthful and are popular with young children, they can also be a source of choking. This hazard can be reduced by cutting the grapes in half or smaller pieces. Also choose snacks that are easily chewed by the children. Limit the amount of sugary foods that are served.

More Background

For further reading and reflection see *Catechism of the Catholic Church* §§ 355–361, 2288–2291; *Compendium—Catechism of the Catholic Church* §§ 66, 474; *United States Catholic Catechism for Adults* pages 389, 390, 422, 423.

Lesson Planner

Faith Focus

God made each of us special. We need to take care of ourselves.

Story

"Shiny Teeth"

Enriching the Lesson

- RCL Benziger *Stories of God's Love* Music CD and companion Songbook, Song 3
- Visit our preschool Web site www.RCLBenzigerPreschool.com this week.

Chapter Objectives

After this week's lesson the children should be able to:

- recall the story "Shiny Teeth."
- share ways that they can take care of themselves.
- thank God for making them special.

Materials Needed

In addition to the general supplies named on page 9 of this guide, you will need the following materials for teaching this lesson:

- copies of activity master on page 156 of this guide, one for each of the children
- pieces of cardboard on which to paste pictures from activity master, one for each of the children
- white crayons or white chalk

Prayer

God, our Creator,
you have given me
the wondrous and precious gift of life.
Guide me to live with great care.
Guide me to always show the children,
by my words and actions,
how precious is the gift of life
you have given them.
Amen.

Shiny Teeth

After Carlos' bubble bath, Mom said, "Doesn't it feel good to be all clean and wrapped in a warm towel? Now you are ready to put on your blue pajamas, the ones that have red trucks all over them. Then you can brush your teeth and get snuggled into bed. And we'll read your *Big Truck* book."

Carlos looked at his mom and said, "Why do I have to brush my teeth? I just brushed them this morning. I want to go to bed now so you can read me my truck book. Come on, Mom. Let's go."

Mom smiled and gave Carlos a big hug. She said, "Let's look in the mirror together. OK? Now smile so I can see all those beautiful white teeth that you have."

Carlos giggled and smiled a big silly smile into the mirror. "Look," Mom said as she pointed to his mouth. "Look at those wonderful white teeth. Brushing keeps them that way. Now guess who gave you those great teeth."

"God gave you teeth," Mom said. "He also gave you eyes, ears, fingers, toes and legs. Every part of you is a special gift from God."

Carlos smiled and said, "Let's brush my teeth, Mom. I think that would make God happy. Don't you?"

Mom said, "Yes, I do, Carlos. It is important that we take care of ourselves."

Carlos answered, "Let's use my favorite toothpaste, the one that smells like bubble gum. I'm going to brush extra well tonight. Then I can go to bed and look at my *Big Truck* book. Come on, Mom. Let's brush!"

Welcome

- Provide copies of the illustrations of the six activities cut from the activity master on page 156 of this guide, each pasted to a piece of cardboard.
- Greet the children by name and direct them to the Welcome Center. Invite a child to select one of the cards and pretend to do the activity on the card. For example, a child running, a child jumping, a child eating an apple, a child sleeping, a child washing their hands, a child drinking water from a glass. Have the other children guess what the child is doing.
- Repeat the activity until all of the children who want to pretend have had their turn.
- Conclude by telling the children, "God made us special. We need to take care of ourselves. When we do these things (hold up cards), we are taking care of ourselves. We need to sleep, exercise and eat healthful foods."

Gather

- Play the gathering song to signal that it is time for the children to clean up and move to the Story Time Area.
- Lead the children in singing song 3 for unit 2 on the *Stories of God's Love* Music CD. Or lead the children in singing the song that you have been singing with the children in chapter 7, chapter 8 and chapter 9 if you are not using the *Stories of God's Love* Music CD and companion Songbook.
- Bring the activity cards to the Story Time Area.

Teach

Introduce the story.

- Show the children the teaching poster or the cover of the children's leaflet for chapter 10. Point to and read the title, "I Take Care of Myself," aloud to the children.
- Recall with the children the activity they did in the Welcome Center by showing them the pictures of the six activities. Invite the children to listen to today's story and discover how Carlos was learning to take care of himself.

Tell the story.

Tell the children the name of today's story, "Shiny Teeth." Refer to the illustration on the teaching poster or the cover of the leaflet as you read the story to the children.

Recall the story

- Help the children recall details of today's story by inviting them to wave both hands in the air if what you say is true.
  —Our story is about Carlos and his shiny teeth. *(True)*
  —Carlos was wearing purple pajamas. *(False)*
  —God gave Carlos his teeth. *(True)*
  —We need to take care of our teeth. *(True)*

- Show the children the pictures of the six activities and point to the illustration of Carlos brushing his teeth. Remind the children that God wants us to take good care of ourselves for we are very special.

 ## Apply

Work on the children's leaflet activity.

- Ask several children to help you hand out the children's leaflet for chapter 10. Have all the children briefly look at the picture on the cover of the leaflet. Recall for them that Carlos was taking care of himself by brushing his teeth.
- Tell the children, "God made your body special. He wants you to take care of your body." Invite the children to name the things they see on the page. Talk about how each takes care of their body. Next have them color a heart below the picture they have done today. Then have them complete the rest at home.

Connect with the child's life.

- Ask the children, "What is one way you will take care of yourself this week?" Invite the children to answer and encourage them to do what they tell you they will try to do.
- Remind the children to take their leaflet home and share the story on the For My Family Page and the activity with their family.

 ## Pray

- Gather the children around the prayer table.
- Lead the children in thanking God for making them special and practice singing the following prayer to the tune of "Mary Had a Little Lamb":

  I am thankful for my teeth, for my teeth, for my teeth.
  I am thankful for my teeth. They are a gift from God.

  Continue singing the song, expressing thanks for "eyes," "legs," "hands" and so on.
- Call the children to a moment of silence. (Pause.) Lead the children in prayer. Begin with the Sign of the Cross.
- Conclude the prayer by leading the children in singing "Amen" to a simple melody.

Additional Activities

Play a "Lassie/Laddie" exercise game.

Use this activity to reinforce the concept that our bodies are special and we should take care of them.

- Remind the children that God made their body and he wants them to keep it healthy. Tell the children that they are going to play a game that will give them exercise.
- Have the children stand in a circle. Tell them that they will play a "Lassie/Laddie" game. The girls will be called "Lassies" and the boys will be called "Laddies." Choose one child to stand in the center of the circle. Explain that the "Lassie" or "Laddie" in the center will do a movement that will exercise their body (demonstrate examples, such as jumping jacks, hopping and so on), and everyone else will sing this song to the tune of "The More We Get Together":

  Did you ever see a Lassie (or Laddie), a Lassie (or Laddie), a Lassie (or Laddie)?
  Did you ever see a Lassie (or Laddie) go this way and that?
  Go this way and that way. And that way and this way.
  Did you ever see a Lassie (or Laddie) go this way and that?
- Once the song is over, the child in the center chooses another child to be the Lassie or Laddie. Repeat the game until all of the children have had a turn.

Complete an exercise obstacle course.

Use this activity to help the children discover that exercise is a fun way to take care of their bodies.

- Set up an age-appropriate obstacle course in a large indoor or outdoor space. Use materials that you have to create the course. Children can climb through boxes, jump over a pillow, climb over or under a table, roll a ball and so on. Be creative, simple and safe.
- Remind the children that God made their bodies and exercise will help keep them healthy. Invite the children to exercise using the obstacle course.

CHAPTER

11 Jesus Is Born

Background
for the Catechist

The Center of God's Loving Plan

The Incarnation of the Son of God is a mystery of faith that we cannot fully understand. The word *incarnation* means "putting on flesh." The Son of God, the second divine Person of the Holy Trinity, became fully human without giving up his divinity. Jesus Christ is fully divine and fully human. He is true God and true man. He is like us in all things but sin.

Through the power of the Holy Spirit, the Virgin Mary conceived and gave birth to her only Son and named him Jesus as the angel requested. Mary is truly the Mother of God because her Son, Jesus, is true God and true man.

In the Bible people's names often describe the role they played in the divine plan of Salvation. The Hebrew name *Jesus* means "God saves." Jesus' very name reveals that he is the Savior of the world.

All of God's promises in the Bible come true in Jesus. He is the One in whom and through whom the divine plan of Salvation would be fulfilled. He is the center and heart of God's loving plan for all humanity.

For Reflection

What are some of the ways that I show others that I believe in Jesus Christ? What can I do this week to help the children live their friendship with Jesus?

About the Children

Throughout this year the children are discovering God's love through hearing and responding to both Bible stories and contemporary stories. The role of storytelling is vital to the emergent literacy development of young children. Through stories children's vocabulary is developed and language structure is enhanced. The story in today's lesson about the birth of Jesus provides an opportunity to share in both the language and faith development of children. This week have the children retell the Bible story of Jesus' birth. Encourage them to talk about what they have learned.

A Few Suggestions . . .

Support the children's natural love of story-telling. Create a quiet reading area in the room. Such a space can be created simply by providing a basket of books in a designated area. Or you might create a reading nook decorated with cushions and a bookshelf with picture books. Make sure the area is always attractive and accessible. Make it a place where every child wants to stop and imagine themselves in the stories.

More Background

For further reading and reflection see *Catechism of the Catholic Church* §§ 456–511, *Compendium—Catechism of the Catholic Church* §§ 85–99, *United States Catholic Catechism for Adults* pages 81–83.

Lesson Planner

Faith Focus

We celebrate the birth of Jesus. Mary is the Mother of Jesus, the Son of God.

Bible Story

"Mary's Baby" (Based on Luke 1:31, 2:3–7)

Enriching the Lesson

- RCL Benziger *Stories of God's Love* Music CD and companion Songbook, Song 4
- Visit our preschool Web site www.RCLBenzigerPreschool.com this week.

Chapter Objectives

After this week's lesson the children should be able to:

- recall the Bible story "Mary's Baby."
- discover that Baby Jesus is the most special baby ever born.
- thank God for giving them Baby Jesus.

Materials Needed

In addition to the general supplies named on page 9 of this guide, you will need the following materials for teaching this lesson:

- copies of activity master on page 157 of this guide, one for each of the children
- closed Bible with bookmark placed at Luke 1:31, 2:3–7
- one piece of blue cloth, two pieces of brown cloth and one piece of white cloth

Prayer

Mary, Mother of Jesus,
Mother of God,
you accepted God's invitation
to become the Mother of Jesus
with deep faith, hope and love.
Pray for me that I might
grow in these virtues
and become a model of holiness
for the children entrusted to my care.
Amen.

Jesus Is Born

Mary's Baby

Long ago in a city named Bethlehem, something very special happened. A special baby whose name was Jesus was born.

Jesus was the most special baby who was ever born. The baby's mother's name was Mary. God the Father chose Mary to be the Mother of his Son, Jesus. God also chose a man named Joseph to care for Mary and Jesus.

Mary and Joseph had to make a special trip when it was near the time Baby Jesus was to be born. They had to go to the city of Bethlehem. Many other people came to Bethlehem at the same time.

When Mary and Joseph arrived there, they knocked on the door of an inn. An inn is a place like a hotel where people can stay when they are on a trip. A man opened the door and told Mary and Joseph, "I have no room for you to stay here. You can stay in the stable where I keep my donkey and other animals."

So Mary and Joseph went to the stable and Jesus was born there. Mary wrapped her baby in soft clothes and placed him in a manger. A manger is a place where the food is put to feed animals.

Mary loved her baby very much. Mary knew her baby was very special. He was the most special baby who was ever born.

BASED ON LUKE 1:31, 2:3–7

76

 ## Welcome

- Provide a set of puzzle pieces for each of the children, made from copies of the activity master found on page 157 of this guide.
- Greet the children by name and direct them to the Welcome Center. Give each of the children a set of puzzle pieces and ask them to put the puzzle pieces together. Show them a completed puzzle to guide them in their work. Walk among the children as they are working and tell them that the picture is about the Bible story that you will tell them today.
- Bring the completed puzzle that you put together before class to the Story Time Area.

 ## Gather

- Play the gathering song to signal that it is time for the children to clean up and move to the Story Time Area.
- Show the children the completed puzzle. Point to the stable in the picture. Explain to the children that a stable is a place where animals are kept and fed. Say the word *stable* out loud again and have the children echo the word *stable* after you.
- Introduce the children to song 4 for unit 3 (chapters 11, 12, 13 and 14) on the *Stories of God's Love* Music CD. Or introduce another appropriate song you and the children will sing during unit 3 if you are not using the *Stories of God's Love* Music CD and companion Songbook. Play the song and let the children listen to the words and melody.

 ## Teach

Introduce the Bible story.

- Display the teaching poster for chapter 11 in the Story Time Area. Show the children the teaching poster or the cover of the children's leaflet. Point to the title "Jesus Is Born" and read it aloud to the children. Then invite the children to talk about what they see in the illustration.
- Ask, "Who would like to hear a Bible story that tells all about the picture?" After the children respond, invite them to listen to the Bible story.

Tell the Bible story.

- Invite a child to come up and open the Bible to the place marked by the bookmark, Luke 1:31, 2:3–7. Take the opened Bible, place the children's leaflet in it and read the Bible story "Mary's Baby " on the For My Family Page to the children.
- Refer to the illustration as you read the Bible story to the children to help them visualize it.

Recall the Bible story.

- Provide a piece of blue cloth, two pieces of brown cloth and a piece of white cloth.

- Have the children dramatize the Bible story. Give the blue cloth to a child to use to play the role of Mary. Give one of the pieces of brown cloth to a child to play the role of Joseph and the other brown cloth to a child to play the role of the innkeeper. Give the white cloth to the child who plays Mary when she pretends to wrap Baby Jesus in soft clothes.
- Read the following parts of the story aloud very slowly so that the children can act them out:
    —Mary and Joseph traveled to Bethlehem. *(Mary and Joseph walk around Story Time Area.)*
    —They came to an inn. *(Mary and Joseph walk to imaginary inn and knock on door.)*
    —A man opened the door of the inn. He told Mary and Joseph, "I have no room for you to stay here. You can stay in the stable." *(Innkeeper pretends to talk to Mary and Joseph and points to stable.)*
    —Mary and Joseph went to the stable. *(Mary and Joseph walk to imaginary stable; perhaps near teacher.)*
    —Jesus was born there and Mary wrapped her baby in soft clothes. *(Mary pretends to wrap Baby Jesus with a piece of white cloth.)*
    —Mary placed Baby Jesus in the manger. *(Mary pretends to place Baby Jesus gently in a manger.)*
- Congratulate the children. Continue retelling and acting out the Bible story as time allows.
- Conclude by telling the children that Baby Jesus was the most special baby ever born. Jesus is the Son of God. Mary is his Mother.

Apply

Work on the children's leaflet activity.

- Ask several children to assist you in handing out the children's leaflet for chapter 11. Have all the children briefly look at the cover of the leaflet to remind them of the Bible story. Ask the children to open their leaflet to the activity pages.
- Read the title aloud to the children. Have the children complete the dot-to-dot activity to discover the picture. Invite them to color the picture. Walk among the children as they are coloring the picture. Remind them that Mary

Jesus, Mary and Joseph Are the Holy Family

Complete the dot-to-dot activity.
Tell the story to a friend.

and Joseph made a trip to the city of Bethlehem and that it was in a stable there that Baby Jesus was born.

Connect with the child's life.

- Give the children their puzzle pieces to take home. Ask them to show the puzzle to their family. Ask, "When you show your puzzle pieces to your family, what will you tell your family about the Baby Jesus?" *(Jesus was born in a stable. Mary is the Mother of Baby Jesus. Jesus is God's Son. Baby Jesus was the most special baby ever born.)*
- Remind the children to take their leaflet home and share the Bible story on the For My Family Page and the activity with their family.

Pray

- Gather the children at the prayer table and quiet them by having them repeat after you, "My head I bow. / My hands I fold. / Now I talk to God." *(Pause.)*
- Have the children echo the words of the prayer after you. Lead the children in prayer. Begin with the Sign of the Cross.

Teacher:	Thank you, God, for Mary.
Children:	*Echo the words.*
Teacher:	Thank you, God, for Joseph.
Children:	*Echo the words.*
Teacher:	Thank you, God, for Baby Jesus.
Children:	*Echo the words.*
Teacher:	Together let us pray, "Amen."
All:	Amen.

Additional Activity

Make Bible bookmarks.

Use this activity to reinforce the concept that the Bible is the holy book of the Church and to help them recall the Bible story about the birth of Jesus.

- Provide washable markers and a stiff piece of paper the size of a bookmark for each of the children on which you have printed the name *JESUS* for them to trace.
- Call attention to the classroom Bible. Tell the children that the Bible is the holy book of the Church that has many stories that tell about Jesus. Have a bookmark placed at Luke 2:7. Open the Bible and read the verse to the children.
- Show the children a "Jesus" bookmark that you have made and remind them how bookmarks are used. Tell the children they are going to make a "Jesus" Bible bookmark.
- Hand out a bookmark to each of the children. Have them use their favorite color marker or crayon and trace the letters to the name *JESUS*.
- Tell the children to take their bookmark home and ask their parents to help them put it in a Bible.

CHAPTER 12

I Have a Family

Background
for the Catechist

The Christian Family

The Christian family is the domestic church, or church of the home. It is the first and primary community of faith into which a child is born and which nurtures a child in faith. The responsibility for educating and nurturing children in faith belongs to the family, primarily to the parents. Faith happens first in families.

Long before children participate in a formal school-based or a parish-based religion program, children are learning and growing in faith at home. From their earliest experiences in their family, children come to know God, hear stories of Jesus and celebrate the Holy Days of the Church.

As children participate in the life of their family, they develop a sense of belonging. This sense of belonging to their immediate family can become the basis and foundation for their developing a sense of belonging to the universal family of believers in Jesus Christ, the Church.

For Reflection

What are some of the things that I have developed the habit of doing on a regular basis to nurture my faith life? What do I do on a regular basis to nurture the faith of the children entrusted to my care?

More Background

For further reading and reflection see *Catechism of the Catholic Church* §§ 1655–1658, 2204–2206, 2221–2230, 2685; *Compendium—Catechism of the Catholic Church* §§ 350, 456, 459–461, 565; *United States Catholic Catechism for Adults* pages 284–286, 373–385.

About the Children

It is common for young children to have new brothers or sisters while they are in preschool. The birth of a new baby is a joyous event for the whole family. Young children, however, often struggle, as their place in the family seems to them to be disrupted. For threes and young fours who thrive on predictable routines, disruptions in family life associated with a new sibling can lead to their irritability as well as regression in areas where they were independent. It is important to help young children see that a new baby in their family does not mean that they are loved any less. Their role as an older sibling is cause for celebration.

A Few Suggestions . . .

Be prepared to celebrate the birth of a new baby into the families of some of the children. When this happens, focus on the role of the child in your class as an older sibling. Celebrate their elevated status of becoming a big brother or sister. Add a sign to the classroom door that says, "Let's Celebrate! *(child's name)* Is a Big Sister!" Have on hand a special "Big Brother" or "Big Sister" crown made out of construction paper, and invite the child to decorate and wear it. At a time when attention is being showered on the new baby at home, religion class can be a place that celebrates the preschooler's role as the older sibling.

Lesson Planner

Faith Focus

We have a family who loves and cares for us. We are happy when a new baby is born into our family.

Story

"A Baby to Love"

Materials Needed

In addition to the general supplies named on page 9 of this guide, you will need the following materials for teaching this lesson:

- construction paper made into crowns
- punch-out figure of Kim, one for each of the children

Enriching the Lesson

- RCL Benziger *Stories of God's Love* Music CD and companion Songbook, Song 4
- Visit our preschool Web site www.RCLBenzigerPreschool.com this week.

Chapter Objectives

After this week's lesson the children should be able to:

- recall the story "A Baby to Love."
- discover that a new baby is a special gift from God to a family.
- thank God for their families.

Prayer

All-loving God,
Father of all,
thank you for the gift of families.
Guide all those
who nurture the faith of children.
Be with me as I share my faith
with the children entrusted to my care.
Amen.

A Baby to Love

Kim had on her favorite new shiny red shoes. Grandma helped her get dressed for this special day. Mommy and Daddy were coming home from the hospital with Kim's new baby sister. Kim was so happy.

Kim couldn't wait to see baby Mya. She hoped, "Maybe Mommy will let me hold the baby if I am very careful."

Everyone was excited. Grandma made a special lunch. Grandpa blew up lots of pink balloons. Mya's crib was all ready for her first nap at home. Seeing the pink and yellow flowered baby blanket in the crib, Kim asked Grandma, "Is that a special blanket for Mya?"

"Yes," Grandma answered. "It is just like the one I made for you. This is a very special day for our family."

"Do you want to sing the song Grandpa and I taught you to sing to baby Mya when she comes home?" Grandma asked.

"Can we practice it again now?" Kim asked Grandma and Grandpa.

"Come over to the piano. Let's practice it one more time," Grandma answered.

Kim had practiced all week and knew all the words. Singing this special song would be Kim's gift to her new baby sister. Mya would know how much Kim loved her. As Grandma began playing the song on the piano, Kim began to sing (*to the tune of "London Bridge"*),

"Baby Mya, welcome home.
Welcome home. Welcome home.
Baby Mya, welcome home.
We all love you."

What a joyful day it was for all of them. Grandma, Grandpa, Mommy, Daddy and Kim were already a family. Now there would be a new baby in the family to love, baby Mya.

 Welcome

- Provide crowns made from construction paper on which you have written each of the children's family name.
- Greet the children by name and direct them to the Welcome Center. Tell the children, "Today we are going to celebrate belonging to a family. I will give each of you a crown to decorate. The name of your family is written on the crown I will give you."
- Hand out the crowns to the children and invite them to use the markers or crayons to decorate their crowns.
- Walk among the children as they are decorating their crowns, address the children by their family names and tell them that God gave each of us a family. Help the children size their crowns by taping the ends so that the crowns fit snugly.
- Tell the children that they will wear their crowns as they listen to the story today.

 Gather

- Play the gathering song to signal that it is time for the children to clean up and move to the Story Time Area. Tell the children to wear their crowns when they go to the Story Time Area.
- Lead the children in singing song 4 for unit 3 on the *Stories of God's Love* Music CD. Or lead the children in singing the song that you selected for this unit (chapters 11, 12, 13 and 14) if you are not using the *Stories of God's Love* Music CD.

 Teach

Introduce the story.

- Show the teaching poster or the cover of the children's leaflet for chapter 11 to the children. Tell them that it is a picture about the Bible story that they heard last time in religion class. Ask, "Who can tell me the names of the people in this picture?" (*Baby Jesus, Mary and Joseph*) Tell them that Jesus, Mary and Joseph were a family.
- Display the teaching poster or show the children the cover of the children's leaflet for chapter 12. Invite the children to listen to discover why Kim and her family were so happy.

Tell the story.

Refer to the teaching poster or the cover of the children's leaflet as you read the story "A Baby to Love" to the children.

Recall the story.

- Call the children's attention to the teaching poster or the cover of the children's leaflet to help them recall the story. Ask:
  —Who were Kim, Grandma and Grandpa waiting for? (*Baby Mya to come home*)

—What special gift was Kim going to give to baby Mya? *(The singing of a special song)*

—Who wants to sing the song to baby Mya with Kim? *(Acknowledge those who answer.)*

■ Invite the children to learn and sing the song to the tune of "London Bridge":

Baby Mya, welcome home.
Welcome home. Welcome home.
Baby Mya, welcome home.
We all love you.

■ Hand out the punch-out figures of Kim to each of the children. Have them hold the figures as they join with you in singing the song. Note: Sing the song with the children several times to help them learn to sing it well.

 ## Apply

Work on the children's leaflet activity.

■ Ask several children to assist you in handing out the children's leaflet for chapter 12. Have all the children look at the cover of the leaflet to help them recall the story about Kim's family.

■ Ask the children to open the leaflet to the activity pages. Read to them the title "What Families Do Together."

■ Talk with the children about each picture and what the family is doing. Invite the children to draw a happy face by the pictures of the things they might like to do with their family. Have the children tell about other things that their families do together that are not shown in the pictures.

■ Walk among the children as they are drawing and remind them that God gave us families.

Connect with the child's life.

■ Ask the children, "What is one thing you will do with your family when you go home today?" Congratulate the children for their responses.

■ Remind the children to take home their leaflet and share the story on the For My Family Page and the activity with their family.

What Families Do Together

Draw a happy face by the things you like to do with your family.
Thank God for your family.

 ## Pray

■ Invite the children to put their crowns on their heads and gather at the prayer table.

■ Tell the children that you are going to tell them the words of today's prayer. Explain that after you pray each part of the prayer you will cross your arms over your heart. Tell them that when you cross your arms over your heart they will pray the words you said quietly in their hearts for only God to hear.

■ Call the children to a moment of silence. *(Pause.)* Lead the children in prayer. Begin with the Sign of the Cross.

Teacher: Dear God, this is *(name)*.
Children: *Pray the words quietly in their heart, saying their name.*
Teacher: Thank you, God, for my family.
Children: *Pray the words quietly in their heart.*
Teacher: God, please bless everyone in my family.
Children: *Pray the words quietly in their heart.*
Teacher: Thank you, God. Amen.
Children: *Pray the words quietly in their heart.*

■ Tell the children to wear their crowns home today.

Additional Activities

Role-play a family.

Use this activity to help the children recall the story.

■ Provide simple props as dress-up clothes, such as an apron, vest, hat, skirt and jacket.

■ Invite the children to help you retell the story. Explain that you will choose children to pretend to be Kim, Grandma and Grandpa. Tell them that you will read parts of the story aloud for each of the characters to act out.

■ Read the chapter story slowly and encourage the children to follow along, acting the different parts out as well as they can.

Pretend play family members taking care of another.

Use this activity to help the children appreciate that members of a family love and care for one another.

■ Provide several small containers with lids that hold a selection of first aid items, such as plastic bandages, cotton balls and wipes; and several dolls, one of each for each group of children.

■ Have the children work in small groups (families). Show the children the containers and ask them to open the containers. Tell them to select items and tell how they might use them to care for their babies.

CHAPTER 13

Shepherds Visit Baby Jesus

Background
for the Catechist

Announcing the Good News of Jesus

Each of us likes to get good news. Good news can turn a bad day into a good day. Good news can lighten a heavy heart and bring light to a dark day.

The shepherds who gathered on that hillside outside of Bethlehem were recipients of the greatest news humanity has received or will have ever received. The angels announced to them, "For today in the city of David a savior has been born for you who is Messiah and Lord" (Luke 2:11).

The shepherds wasted no time in responding to the good news of the angels. Upon hearing the news, they left their sheep and went with haste to find the Savior. Not only did they go and find the Savior they also announced the Good News of the Savior's birth to others!

As Christians we are called to take part in the Church's work of evangelization. We are to announce the Good News of Jesus to others. We announce that Good News when we give witness to Jesus Christ and the Gospel by our words and actions. Announcing this Good News is at the heart of the work of all the baptized. It is the mission of the Church, the Body of Christ.

For Reflection

What have I done and continue to do that gives witness to my faith in Jesus, the Savior of the world? What can I do this week to help the children tell their families about Jesus?

About the Children

Children this age learn best in creative-play situations in which they have an opportunity to try out new skills and learn the language associated with these new skills. Children tend to engage in everyday life scenarios in their play and often role-play negative as well as positive characteristics of people. Children also love to hear and tell stories. Tell the Gospel stories with enthusiasm. The children will catch that enthusiasm and want to share the stories you tell them with their families.

A Few Suggestions . . .

Create an atmosphere of enthusiasm for reading and telling the stories. Provide the children opportunities to dramatize the stories. Let them take turns playing the role of the characters in the story. Provide simple props, such as pieces of cloth for clothes. Join in the play with the children. Refer to the different qualities of the characters in the story. This can be an effective way to help the children discover positive and negative traits, and aspire to imitate the positive behavior traits and decide not to imitate the negative traits.

More Background

For further reading and reflection see *Catechism of the Catholic Church* §§ 422–429, 849–856, 905; *Compendium—Catechism of the Catholic Church* §§ 79, 80, 172, 173, 190; *United States Catholic Catechism for Adults* pages 117–118 and 135–136.

Lesson Planner

Faith Focus

Shepherds told others about Baby Jesus.

Bible Story

"Shepherds Hear Good News" (Based on Luke 2:8–20)

Enriching the Lesson

- RCL Benziger *Stories of God's Love* Music CD and companion Songbook, Song 4
- Visit our preschool Web site www.RCLBenzigerPreschool.com this week.

Chapter Objectives

After this week's lesson the children should be able to:

- recall the Bible story "Shepherds Hear Good News."
- discover that Jesus' birth was good news to the shepherds.
- thank God for Baby Jesus.

Materials Needed

In addition to the general supplies named on page 9 of this guide, you will need the following materials for teaching this lesson:

- black construction paper, one sheet for each of the children
- white chalk, one piece for each of the children
- closed Bible with bookmark placed at Luke 2:8–20

Prayer

Lord God, you are Father of all.
Thank you for sending your Son, Jesus,
to be the Savior of all people.
Strengthen me to spread that Good News
and guide me to help the children
come to know Jesus.
Amen.

13 Shepherds Visit Baby Jesus

Stories of God's Love
Ages 3 and 4

Shepherds Hear Good News

Soon after Jesus was born, God sent angels to some shepherds. The shepherds were near the place where Jesus was born and were taking care of their sheep. It was nighttime and very dark. *(Have the children hold up and look at their drawings.)*

Then the shepherds saw a bright light. They became afraid because they didn't know what was happening.

Then they heard an angel say to them, "Do not be afraid. I have good news from God for you. The news will make everyone happy."

The angel then told the shepherds the good news. The angel said, "A special baby has been born. He is the special baby who God promised would be born. Go to Bethlehem. You will find him lying in a manger."

The shepherds said to one another, "Let's hurry to the city of Bethlehem to find the baby in the manger." They followed the bright star until they found Mary and Joseph and Baby Jesus. He was lying in a manger just as the angel told them.

The shepherds were so happy and excited that they told everyone what had happened. They told everyone, "The Savior who God promised to send has been born in Bethlehem. We have seen him."

BASED ON LUKE 2:8–20

 Welcome

- Display the teaching poster of chapter 13 in the Welcome Center or have on hand the children's leaflet for this chapter. Provide sheets of black construction paper and pieces of white chalk, one for each of the children.
- Greet the children by name and direct them to the Welcome Center. Show them the teaching poster or the cover of the children's leaflet for this chapter. Invite the children to tell you what they see in the picture. *(Shepherds are visiting with Baby Jesus in the nighttime.)*
- Show the children the black construction paper and the white chalk and explain the activity to them. Tell them the black paper is dark like the night sky. They can use the white chalk to draw bright stars to light up the sky. (Note: Remember that young children's art may not look like what they say they have drawn.) Praise their creativity.
- Conclude by helping them put their name on their paper.

 Gather

- Play the gathering song to signal that it is time for the children to clean up and move to the Story Time Area.
- Have the children bring their drawings to the Story Time Area.
- Lead the children in singing song 4 for unit 3 on the *Stories of God's Love* Music CD. Or lead the children in singing the song that you have selected for unit 3 (chapters 11, 12, 13 and 14) if you are not using the *Stories of God's Love* Music CD.

 Teach

Introduce the Bible story.

- Bring the teaching poster and children's leaflet for chapter 13 to the Story Time Area.
- Call the children's attention to the teaching poster or the cover of the children's leaflet.
- Tell the children, "We all like to hear good news." Give examples of good news that children like to hear. For example, their grandmother and grandfather are coming for a visit, it's snack time and so on.
- Ask the children to listen for the good news the shepherds heard as you read the Bible story to them.

Tell the Bible story.

Invite a child to come up and open the Bible to the place marked by the bookmark, Luke 2:8–20. Take the opened Bible, place the children's leaflet inside and read the Bible story "Shepherds Hear Good News" on the For My Family Page to the children. Refer to the teaching poster or the cover of the children's leaflet as you read the Bible story.

Recall the Bible story.

■ Help the children recall the details of today's Bible story by asking them to answer some questions. Tell the children to hold up their drawings of the stars and say, "It was nighttime and dark outside. The shepherds saw a very bright light that made the darkness go away." Ask:
  —Who came to the shepherds? *(an angel)*
  —Who sent the angel to the shepherds? *(God)*
  —What was the good news from God that the angel told the shepherds? *(a special baby was born)*
  —Who was the special baby? *(Jesus)*

■ Summarize by reminding the children that after the shepherds visited with Baby Jesus, they told everyone the good news about Baby Jesus, the Savior who God promised to send.

 ## Apply

Work on the children's leaflet activity.

■ Ask several children to help you hand out the children's leaflet for chapter 13. Tell all the children to briefly look at the cover of the leaflet to help them recall the Bible story "Shepherds Hear Good News."

■ Tell the children to open their leaflet and look at the activity. Read the title "Help the Shepherds" aloud to the children and explain the activity to them.

■ Tell the children that they are going to help the shepherds find Baby Jesus. Ask the children to touch the picture of the shepherds with their pointer finger and use their finger to follow the path from the shepherds to Baby Jesus in the manger.

■ Next invite the children to use a crayon or marker to mark the path from the shepherds to Baby Jesus. Finally, invite the children to finish coloring the illustration.

■ Walk among the children as they are coloring the picture. Remind the children that the shepherds told everyone about Baby Jesus.

Connect with the child's life.

■ Ask the children what they will tell their families about the shepherds' visit to Baby Jesus when they go home today.

Help the Shepherds

Follow the path to Jesus. Color the picture.
Tell a friend about the picture.

■ Remind the children to take home their drawings and their leaflet and share the Bible story on the For My Family Page and the activity with their family.

 ## Pray

■ Gather the children around the prayer table.

■ Introduce the prayer by telling the children to echo the words "Thank you, God" after you. Call them to a moment of silence. *(Pause.)* Lead the children in prayer. Begin with the Sign of the Cross.

Teacher: For Baby Jesus, thank you, God.
Children: *Echo the words* "Thank you, God."
Teacher: For Mary and Joseph, thank you, God.
Children: *Echo the words* "Thank you, God."
Teacher: Together let us pray, "Amen."
All: Amen.

Additional Activities

Make "Good News" announcements.

Use this activity to reinforce the concept that Jesus' birth is good news.

■ Provide samples of announcements that you have received in the mail, crayons or washable markers or crayons and pieces of paper on which you have written the announcement "GOOD NEWS! JESUS IS BORN." Write the words "GOOD NEWS!" and "IS BORN" in brightly colored letters. Write the name *JESUS* in larger letters than "GOOD NEWS" and "IS BORN" and in dots or dashes that the children can trace.

■ Show the children a sample of a one-page announcement that the religion program or school has already sent home. Explain that they will make announcements to tell others the good news that Jesus is born.

■ Hand out the announcement sheets and explain the activity to the children. Tell the children that they will take home their announcements to give to their families.

Role-play the Bible story.

Use this activity to help the children remember and retell the Bible story.

■ Provide blocks in the Dramatic Play Area on which you have glued images of Mary, Joseph, Baby Jesus in a manger, shepherds, a donkey and sheep.

■ Invite the children to use the blocks to retell the Bible story to one another.

CHAPTER 14

A Visit from My Family

Background
for the Catechist

The Cradle of Faith

Jesus was born into and grew up in a loving family that worshiped God and celebrated the teachings and traditions of the Jewish faith. In the Holy Family Jesus lived and "advanced [in] wisdom and age and favor before God and man" (Luke 2:52) as he prepared to accomplish the work his Father sent him to do.

The Christian family is the cradle of faith for all of the baptized. It is within the Christian family, the domestic church, that children begin their journey of development as faith-filled persons. Children learn from their parents and other family members that their first calling as a Christian is to follow Jesus Christ.

Parents care for the spiritual and physical needs of their children. They help and guide their children to discover their talents, to discern and prepare for the way of life the Holy Spirit is calling them to follow. Catechists support Catholic parents and families in fulfilling these responsibilities.

For Reflection

What are some of the ways my family supported me in discerning the way God calls me to live my faith? What can I do to support the families who have entrusted their children to my care to guide their children in the way of faith?

About the Children

Children of all ages enjoy parties and celebrations. They can bring much joy and excitement to young children. The activities and the meeting of new people often associated with parties and celebrations can challenge threes and fours. Unfamiliar routines, new people and unpredictability can lead to high levels of frustration because young children usually feel more comfortable and secure with the predictable and the known. Parties and celebrations are also opportunities for children to learn how to properly express their feelings of excitement and adapt to new situations.

A Few Suggestions . . .

One way to help children manage their feelings is to talk about what is happening when they get overly excited. Give the children the opportunity to talk about their feelings before they become too intense. It is important to maintain a calm, predictable environment. If the children's routine is going to change, talk with them about what they might expect. Help reduce their feelings of frustration by planning activities and using materials that will give the children the opportunity to experience a high degree of success.

More Background

For further reading and reflection see *Catechism of the Catholic Church* §§ 512–518, 531–534, 2214–2231; *Compendium—Catechism of the Catholic Church* §§ 101, 104, 459–461; *United States Catholic Catechism for Adults* pages 79–87, 377–379.

Lesson Planner

Faith Focus

We are happy when our family visits.

Story

"The Birthday Visit"

Materials Needed

In addition to the general supplies named on page 9 of this guide, you will need the following materials for teaching this lesson:

- stickers

Enriching the Lesson

- RCL Benziger *Stories of God's Love* Music CD and companion Songbook, Song 4
- Visit our preschool Web site www.RCLBenzigerPreschool.com this week.

Chapter Objectives

After this week's lesson the children should be able to:

- recall the story "The Birthday Visit."
- discover the joy of a visit from our families.
- ask God to bless their families.

Prayer

God, our Father,
send your blessings
on my family
and on the families
of the children in my care.
Amen.

The Birthday Visit

Abby was four years old today. Mom had baked and decorated a very special cake. But the best part was that Grandma and Grandpa were coming to visit. They lived far away, and Mom said they would be staying for the night. This was going to be the best day ever!

Abby loved her Grandma and Grandpa very much. She loved sitting in their laps and playing with them. She especially liked when they tucked her into bed and when Grandpa told her stories about when he was her age.

"Mom," she called into the kitchen. "When will Grandma and Grandpa be here? I wish they would hurry!"

Mom came into the living room, and smiling, she said, "They'll be here very soon. Why don't you play with your doll until they get here?"

Abby sat down on the floor and just as she picked up her doll, she heard the doorbell ring. Jumping up, Abby ran to the window, looked out and called out in a happy voice, "Mom, hurry. Grandma and Grandpa are here. Hurry, Mommy!"

Mom quickly came into the room and opened the door. There stood Grandpa and Grandma with big smiles.

Jumping up and down, Abby called out, "Grandma, Grandpa, it's my birthday. I'm four today!" She jumped into Grandma's arms, and, after a big hug, Grandpa took her into his arms for a squeeze and a kiss.

Taking the hands of Grandpa and Grandma, she led them into the kitchen saying, "Grandma, come. Come with Grandpa and me. See my special birthday cake. It's for my birthday party. Mom made it just for me!"

Abby gave them both another big hug. She was smiling and so happy. Grandma and Grandpa's visits were the best thing ever.

 ## Welcome

- Display the teaching poster for chapter 14 in the Welcome Center or have on hand the children's leaflet for this chapter.
- Greet the children by name and direct them to the Welcome Center. Show them the teaching poster or children's leaflet for this chapter. Invite the children to tell you what they see in the picture. *(Abby's grandparents are visiting her.)* Explain that families welcome family members, friends and other visitors when they come to their home to visit them.
- Talk with the children about how you welcome each of them by name each time they come to religion class. Now invite the children to greet by name one person close to them, gently shaking their hand and saying, "Hello, I am happy that you are in our class."

 ## Gather

- Play the gathering song to signal that it is time for the children to clean up and move to the Story Time Area.
- Lead the children in singing song 4 for unit 3 on the *Stories of God's Love* Music CD. Or lead the children in singing the song that you selected for unit 3 if you are not using the *Stories of God's Love* Music CD.

 ## Teach

Introduce the story.

- Show the children the teaching poster or the cover of the children's leaflet for chapter 14. Point to Abby in the picture and ask the children to tell you her name.
- Have the children echo the word *Welcome* after you. Tell them that you will read a story to them about Abby and the special people she welcomed. Ask them to listen as you read the story to find out who Abby welcomed and what she did to welcome her special visitors.

Tell the story.

Tell the children the title of the story "The Birthday Visit." Read the story to the children. Refer to the teaching poster or to the cover of the children's leaflet as you read the story "The Birthday Visit" to the children.

Recall the story.

- Help the children recall details of today's story. Explain that you will tell them five things about the story. Tell them to hold up their hand if what you say is true. Demonstrate the activity by reading the first statement aloud. Then hold up your hand and ask the children to hold up their hands.

  —Our story is about Abby. *(Yes)*

- Continue the activity. Add additional statements if you wish.
  —Abby was having a birthday party. *(Yes)*
  —Abby's friends at school came to visit her on her birthday. *(No)*
  —Abby's Grandma and Grandpa came to visit her on her birthday. *(Yes)*
  —Abby was so happy. *(Yes)*
- Summarize by reminding the children that Abby thought Grandma and Grandpa's visits were the best thing ever.

Apply

Work on the children's leaflet activity.

- Ask several children to help you hand out the children's leaflet for chapter 14. Have all the children briefly look at the cover of the leaflet. Recall for them how Abby's grandparents came to visit Abby on her birthday.
- Ask the children to open the children's leaflet to the activity pages. Read the title of the activity "Welcome to My Home" aloud to the children. Have them point to the word *Welcome* and say it aloud after you several times.
- Remind the children that families are glad when people visit them. Explain the directions to the activity and ask them to color in the spaces and create the welcome sign.
- Walk among the children as they are drawing their pictures and tell them that we welcome people into our homes when we do happy things with people who visit us.

Connect with the child's life.

- Ask the children,
  —Who are some people who come to visit you in your home?
  —What do you do to welcome people who come to your home to visit you and your family?

  Give clues to help the children respond. For example, you might tell them some of the people you invite and the things that you do.

- Congratulate the children for their responses with such statements as, "What a great idea!" (Smile at them, clap your hands and so on).
- Remind the children to take their leaflet home and share the story on the For My Family Page and activity with their family. Tell them to ask their parents to hang their "Welcome" banner on the front door of their home.

Pray

- Gather the children at the prayer table.
- Ask the children to think of people who they want to pray for. *(Pause.)*
- Tell the children to name the people out loud when you give them the signal. Call the children to a moment of silence. *(Pause.)* Lead them in prayer. Begin with the Sign of the Cross.

Teacher:	Let us ask God to bless the people in our families. God, bless the people in our families. *Invite the children to say out loud the names of the people who they want to pray for.*
Children:	*Say names out loud.*
Teacher:	*Invite the children to pray quietly in their hearts for anyone else in their family who they want to pray for.*
Children:	*Say names quietly.*
Teacher:	Together, let us pray, "Thank you, God, for our families. Amen."
All:	Thank you, God, for our families. Amen.

Additional Activity

Pretend play our family receiving visitors.

Use this activity to help the children discover the joy of a visit from members of their family.

- Provide several puppets of people (parents, grandparents, young people), enough to represent a family, and a puppet stage made out of a large box. Create your own simple puppets out of poster board if you do not have puppets. Glue tongue depressors or ice cream sticks as handles to the backs of the shapes you have created.
- Invite the children to go to the Dramatic Play Area or wherever you have set up the puppet stage. Have them name and use the puppets to pretend play a visit from members of their family.

CHAPTER 15

Friends of Jesus

Background
for the Catechist

The Call to Discipleship

In today's lesson we find Jesus inviting Peter, Andrew, James and John to follow him. Through their friendship with Christ the disciples came to know the depth of God's love for them. They discovered how to respond to God's invitation to know and believe in him, to place their hope in him, to love him above all else and to love one another and others because of their love for God.

Jesus also invites us to be his disciples—his followers and friends. Empowered by the Holy Spirit we respond in faith to Christ's invitation to be his disciples and friends and to be one with him and his Father through the power of the Holy Spirit. (See John 17:22.) At Baptism we are joined to Christ, receive the gift of the Holy Spirit and are initiated into the community of his followers, the Body of Christ, the Church.

Living as a disciple of Christ is not a one-time decision. It is a decision the Holy Spirit calls and strengthens us to make over and over, each day of our lives, ever deepening our relationship with Christ and in him with the Father and the Holy Spirit. Through our relationship with Christ—through our communion and intimacy with him—we experience the love of Christ who calls us his friends. (See John 15:15.)

For Reflection

In what ways does my life reflect that I am living as a disciple and friend of Jesus? What can I do this week to help the children discover that Jesus invites them to be his friends?

About the Children

Adults are often fascinated—even surprised—by the dramatic increase in vocabulary that occurs with three- and young four-year-olds. When parents and other adults witness threes and young fours using their growing vocabulary, they need to avoid jumping to the conclusion that such increased vocabulary automatically brings about an ability to cooperate better with peers and more accurately express their feelings.

A Few Suggestions . . .

Feelings impact the way we relate (cooperate) with others. While the vocabulary of threes and fours is increasing, they still lack the language to accurately express their feelings. Children benefit greatly from adults who talk about how actions make them feel. While it may seem quicker and easier to resolve disputes between children, it is more beneficial to help them accurately express their feelings about what is happening. Bring the children involved in a "conflict" situation together, saying, "Tell Sue how it makes you feel when she takes your toy. Tell Sue, 'I would like my toy back. You can play with it when I'm done.'" Such an approach will help children learn the skills to resolve conflicts respectfully.

More Background

For further reading and reflection see *Catechism of the Catholic Church* §§ 142–165, 520, 618, 767, 1427–1429; *Compendium—Catechism of the Catholic Church* §§ 25–28; *United States Catholic Catechism for Adults* pages 6–7, 37–41.

Lesson Planner

Faith Focus

Jesus invites four fishermen to be his special friends. We are also friends of Jesus.

Bible Story

"Come, Follow Me" (Based on Matthew 4:18–22)

Materials Needed

In addition to the general supplies named on page 9 of this guide, you will need the following materials for teaching this lesson:

- different colors of play dough or soft clay
- small cookie cutters in the shape of fish
- closed Bible with bookmark placed at Matthew 4:18–22

Enriching the Lesson

- RCL Benziger *Stories of God's Love* Music CD and companion Songbook, Song 5
- Visit our preschool Web site www.RCLBenzigerPreschool.com this week.

Chapter Objectives

After this week's lesson the children should be able to:

- recall the Bible story "Come, Follow Me."
- explain that they are friends of Jesus.
- thank God for their friends.

Prayer

Lord Jesus,
I have heard your invitation,
"Come, follow me."
Peter, Andrew, James and John
helped you spread the good news
of God's love for us.
Send the Holy Spirit to guide me
to share that good news with the children.
Amen.

15 Friends of Jesus

Stories of God's Love
Ages 3 and 4

"Come, Follow Me."

One day Jesus was walking beside a very large lake. He saw two fishermen in their boat. They were throwing their nets into the water trying to catch some fish. The fishermen were brothers. Their names were Peter and Andrew.

Jesus said to Peter and Andrew, "Come, follow me."

The two brothers dropped their nets and followed Jesus. As Jesus, Peter and Andrew walked along, they came to two other fishermen. They were in their boat with their father fixing a tear in their fishing net. Their names were James and John.

Jesus said to James and John, "Come, follow me." The two brothers dropped their net, climbed out of their boat and followed Jesus.

Peter, Andrew, James and John became Jesus' very special friends. Jesus would give them the job of telling people about him.

BASED ON MATTHEW 4:18–22

Welcome

- Provide play dough or soft clay in a variety of colors and small cookie cutters in the shape of fish.
- Greet the children by name and direct them to the Welcome Center. Show them a fish shape that you made out of play dough. Invite them to use the play dough or soft clay to make their own fish shapes.
- Walk among the children as they are making their fish, and tell them that the Bible story they will hear today tells about four fishermen.

Gather

- Play the gathering song to signal that it is time for the children to clean up and move to the Story Time Area. Suggest to the children that they work with a friend as a clean-up helper.
- Have the children bring their fish with them and have the "friends" who helped each other clean up sit beside each other in the Story Time Area.
- Introduce song 5 for unit 4 (chapters 15, 16, 17 and 18) on the *Stories of God's Love* Music CD and Songbook to the children. Or introduce the children to an appropriate song that you will sing with them during unit 4 if you are not using the *Stories of God's Love* Music CD and Songbook.

Teach

Introduce the Bible story.

- Show the children the teaching poster or the cover of the children's leaflet for this chapter. Point to the title "Friends of Jesus" and read it aloud to the children.
- Have the children look at their fish. Invite them to listen to the Bible story to discover the names of four fishermen Jesus called to be his very special friends.

Tell the Bible story.

- Invite a child to come up and open the Bible to the page marked by the bookmark, Matthew 4:18–22.
- Take the opened Bible, place the children's leaflet inside. Tell the children the name of the Bible story "Come, Follow Me." Refer to the teaching poster or the cover of the children's leaflet as you read the Bible story on the For My Family Page to the children.

Recall the Bible story.

- Help the children recall the Bible story by having them learn and clap along as they sing this song to the tune of "Mary Had a Little Lamb."

    Jesus said, "Come, follow me, follow me, follow me."
        Jesus said, "Come, follow me. I call you special friends."

Andrew, Peter, James and John, Andrew and Peter,
James and John,
Andrew, Peter, James and John are Jesus' special friends.

■ Sing the song several times with the children.

 Apply

Work on the children's leaflet activity.

■ Ask several children to help you hand out the children's leaflet for chapter 15. Have all the children briefly look at the cover of the leaflet. Recall with them the names of the people that Jesus called to be his very special friends.

■ Ask the children to open the children's leaflet to the activity. Ask them to tell you what they see.

■ Point to and have the children look at the title on the page. Read the title aloud and explain the activity to the children. Invite the children to pretend that they are with the children in the picture and they hear Jesus calling to them, "Come! Be My Friend." Invite them to respond to Jesus and go to him by drawing a line on the path.

■ Walk among the children as they are working on the activity and tell them that Jesus wants them to be his friends.

Connect with the child's life.

■ Ask the children, "Who can you tell at home that you are a friend of Jesus?" Conclude by telling the children, "Isn't it wonderful that we are friends of Jesus!"

■ Remind the children to take their leaflet home and share the Bible story on the For My Family Page and the activity with their family.

 Pray

■ Gather the children at the prayer table.

■ Tell the children that they will sing the prayer today. Explain to them that they will use the song they sang to the melody to "Mary Had a Little Lamb," but they will use their names in place of the names, Andrew, Peter, James and John. Demonstrate one verse of the song, using four of the children's names.

■ Practice the prayer with the children.
Jesus said, "Come, follow me, follow me, follow me."
Jesus said, "Come, follow me. I call you all my friends."

Come! Be My Friend!

Jesus invites you to be his friend.
Follow the path to Jesus.

Name 1, Name 2, Name 3 and Name 4, Name 1 and
Name 2, Name 3 and Name 4,
Name 1, Name 2, Name 3 and Name 4, they all are
Jesus' friends.

■ Add verses until all the names of the children are included in the prayer. Quiet the children by having them repeat after you, "My head I bow. / My hands I fold. / Now I talk to God."

■ Lead them in prayer. Begin with the Sign of the Cross. Conclude by praying "Amen" aloud with the children.

Additional Activities

Paint a lake scene.

Use this activity to help the children relate to the lake setting of today's Bible story.

■ Provide different colors of washable paints and large pieces of heavy paper.

■ Show the children the teaching poster or the cover of the children's leaflet. Remind the children that Jesus was walking along a large lake. Jesus saw Andrew, Peter, James and John in their fishing boats on the lake. He called out to them and asked them to follow him.

■ Invite the children to paint a picture of a large lake and what they might find in and around the lake.

■ Walk among the children as they are drawing and remind them that in today's story Jesus chose four special helpers to be his friends and to help him tell people how much God loves people.

Play a letter-match game.

Use this activity to help the children learn the names of Jesus' special friends, Peter, Andrew, James and John.

■ Provide name plates with one of the names *Peter, Andrew, James* or *John* on each. Print each name in a different color. Also provide ten 3-inch by 5-inch index cards cut in half with a single letter from each of the four names on each. Copy each letter and color as on the name plate.

■ Place the name plates in one grouping. Mix up all the single-letter cards face down on a table. Organize the children in work groups of up to four players.

■ Explain the activity and guide the children in playing the game: One child chooses one of the name plates. Children take turns turning over one of the letter cards. If the selected card matches the color and a letter on their name plate, the child keeps the card and play moves on to the next person. If the card does not match, the child gets to turn the card back over and choose until there is a match. Play continues until everyone has matched all the letters on their name plate.

CHAPTER 16

I Am a Friend of Jesus

Background
for the Catechist

Churches: Testimonies of Faith

The Church is, first and foremost, the community of the baptized gathered together by God in the name of Christ. Celebrating the three Sacraments of Christian Initiation—Baptism, Confirmation and Eucharist—joins us to Christ and makes us full members of the Body of Christ, the Church. We receive the gift of the Holy Spirit and are made sharers in God's life and receive the grace to live as adopted children of God the Father and friends and followers of Jesus Christ.

We also use the name *church* to identify the place where Christians gather in Christ's name to worship God and proclaim the Good News of his love for all people. Throughout the ages Christians have given witness to their faith through the building of churches. For the first Christians, their churches were their homes. This remained the case for the first three centuries because Christianity was considered a "subversive" religion by the leaders of the Roman Empire. In the fourth century after Emperor Constantine granted Christians the right to worship publicly, Christians built places, or basilicas, where they gathered, primarily for worship. Today, landscapes around the world are marked by these great testimonies of faith.

For Reflection

What are some of the ways that I invite others to come to know God's love for them? What can I do this week to help the children grow in their identity as followers and friends of Jesus?

More Background

For further reading and reflection see *Catechism of the Catholic Church* §§ 751–757, 787–791, 946–953, 1145–1158, 1179–1186; *Compendium—Catechism of the Catholic Church* §§ 147–148, 156, 194, 236–240, 244–246; *United States Catholic Catechism for Adults* pages 125–139.

About the Children

An important aspect of a child's development is the development of their aesthetic sense, or their sense of beauty. Aesthetic development is fostered through a child's experience of art, music and movement. Children also develop their aesthetic sense when parents and teachers and other adults call their attention to artistic representations in their environment. Children who are not yet reading or writing use simple artistic expression, such as drawing, to communicate their knowledge and to demonstrate a skill that they have successfully learned. The manner in which teachers engage children in art projects, such as drawing, coloring and dramatic play, contributes significantly to a child's ability to discover, learn and successfully demonstrate their new-found knowledge and skills.

A Few Suggestions . . .

Help the children become focused observers. Before involving children in the performance of artistic activities, spend time exploring the particular subject of the project. For example, point out the textures, shapes, colors, sounds and movements associated with the project. Christians express their faith through the beauty of art which can be fascinating to young children. Take the children on a walking tour of the church. The beauty displayed in the church provides children with a wide variety of sensory and artistic experiences.

Lesson Planner

Faith Focus

We are friends of Jesus. We come together in our church.

Story

"The Remember Game"

Enriching the Lesson

- RCL Benziger *Stories of God's Love* Music CD and companion Songbook, Song 5
- Visit our preschool Web site www.RCLBenzigerPreschool.com this week.

Chapter Objectives

After this week's lesson the children should be able to:

- recall the story "The Remember Game."
- identify the different things they see in the church.
- thank God for beautiful churches.

Materials Needed

In addition to the general supplies named on page 9 of this guide, you will need the following materials for teaching this lesson:

- clear Contact®, or similar paper
- several bright colors of tissue paper cut into shapes
- punch-out figures of Jamal, one for each of the children

Prayer

Gracious God,
the beauty of the world you created
reminds us of your goodness and love for us.
May my words and actions
remind the children
of your love for them.
Amen.

The Remember Game

On the way home from church one Sunday, Jamal and his family decided to play a game in the car.

Dad said, "Let's play 'The Remember Game.' We will each name one thing we remember about church. Let's see what we can remember."

Jamal loved "The Remember Game." "Can I go first?" he asked. He was very excited.

Mom answered, "OK, Jamal. You go first."

"I remember the windows. They are so pretty. The glass is red and blue and yellow and green."

"Good one," said Dad. "Now it's my turn. I remember the long aisle down the middle with rows of seats on both sides. I like the way we can choose which side to sit on each week."

"Let's see," said Mom. "I remember the candles on the altar."

It was Jamal's turn again. He thought for a minute about what he remembered. "I know. I remember all the people in the church. I like the people."

Mom looked into the back seat and smiled at Jamal. She said, "I like the people too. We are all friends of Jesus."

"I can't wait to go to church again," said Jamal. "I'm going to look for more things to name the next time we play 'The Remember Game.'"

 ## Welcome

- Provide sheets of clear Contact® or similar type of paper and a variety of shapes cut from tissue paper of a variety of colors as well as a completed stained-glass window that you have made using tissue paper.
- Greet the children by name and direct them to the Welcome Center. Remind the children that last week they learned that we are all friends of Jesus. Tell the children that the friends of Jesus go to church every Sunday. Say the word *church* aloud and invite the children to echo the word *church* after you.
- Explain to the children that when they go to church they will see many beautiful things. Point out that they can see the altar and the cross, the statues and the colored windows with the sunlight shining through them. Tell the children that these windows are called stained-glass windows.
- Show the children the stained-glass window you made. Invite the children to make stained-glass windows and give them directions for the activity.
- Give each of the children a piece of clear Contact® or similar type of paper with the sticky surface facing upward. Tell the children to place the tissue paper shapes onto the sticky surface. Show them how to overlap the shapes to make new colors. Cover their work with another sheet of clear Contact® or similar type of paper when they have finished using the tissue paper. These works of art can be hung in the classroom or taken home for display.
- Walk among the children as they are working and tell them that all the beautiful things we see and hear in church remind us that God is good and always loves us.

 ## Gather

- Play the gathering song to signal that it is time for the children to clean up and move to the Story Time Area.
- Lead the children in singing song 5 for unit 4 on the *Stories of God's Love* Music CD that you taught them last time. Or lead the children in singing the song that you selected for this unit if you are not using the *Stories of God's Love* Music CD and Songbook.

 ## Teach

Introduce the story.

Show the children the teaching poster or the cover of the children's leaflet for chapter 16. Tell them that today's lesson is about our church family. Invite the children to listen to a story to discover what Jamal and his family remember seeing at church.

Tell the story.

Tell the children the name of the story "The Remember Game." Refer to the teaching poster or the cover of the children's leaflet as you read the story to the children.

Recall the story.

- Help the children recall details of today's story by inviting them to play a remember game about the story. Hand out the punch-out figures of Jamal to each of the children. Ask the children to raise the figure of Jamal in the air if what you tell them about the story is true.
    - —Jamal and his family played a remember game. *(True)*
    - —Jamal and his family were walking home from church when they played "The Remember Game." *(No)*
    - —They were in their car driving home when they played "The Remember Game." *(True)*
    - —Each person named something they remembered seeing in church. *(True)*
    - —Jamal first remembered the windows. *(True)*
    - —Jamal then remembered the people he saw in church. *(True)*
- Summarize by reminding the children that church is a special place where the friends of Jesus come together. There are many beautiful things inside a church that remind us that God is good and always loves us.

Apply

Work on the children's leaflet activity.

- Ask several children to help you hand out the children's leaflet for chapter 16. Have the children briefly look at the cover and help them recall the story.
- Tell the children to open the leaflet to the activity pages. Call the children's attention to the words "I Like Going to Church" and read them aloud to the children.
- Tell the children that the pictures on the page are pictures of some things we see in church. Help the children name what they see.
- Talk with the children about the things they like to see in church.

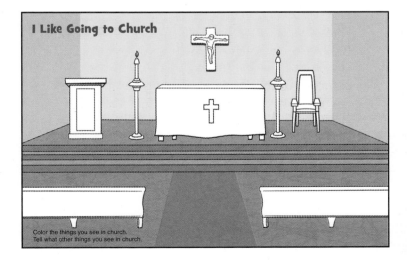

I Like Going to Church

Color the things you see in church.
Tell what other things you see in church.

Connect with the child's life.

- Invite the children to name the things that they remember seeing or hearing in church. Invite them to play a remember game about church with their families as they go home today.
- Remind the children to take their leaflet home and share the story and the activity with their family.

Pray

- Gather the children around the prayer table. Tell the children they will echo the words of the prayer after you.
- Call them to a moment of silence. *(Pause.)* Lead the children in praying this or a similar prayer thanking God for all the things we see or hear in church. Begin with the Sign of the Cross.

Teacher: Let us thank God for our beautiful church. Thank you, God, for our church.
Children: *Echo the words of the prayer.*
Teacher: Thank you, God, for the windows in our church.
Children: *Echo the words of the prayer.*
Teacher: Thank you, God, for *(name other things the children see or hear.)*
Children: *Echo the words of the prayer.*
Teacher: Thank you, God, for all the people in our church.
Children: *Echo the words of the prayer.*
Teacher: Together let us pray, "Amen."
All: Amen.

Additional Activity

Build a church.

Use this activity to reinforce the children's understanding of churches as beautiful buildings that remind us of God's love.

- Provide glue or paste, crayons and washable markers, sheets of construction paper, and pre-cut shapes made from construction paper, triangles for the roof, squares or rectangles for the body, small squares for windows and a cross for the top.
- Show the children a church that you constructed using the construction paper shapes. Invite the children to create their own church by gluing the pieces together on a larger piece of paper.
- Optional: Display several different pictures of churches to give the children an idea of what the outside of churches look like.
- Walk among the children as they are building their churches and remind them that Christians build churches to show their love for God.

CHAPTER 17

Jesus Has Many Friends

Background
for the Catechist

The Work of the Church

Matthew's Gospel concludes with the Risen Jesus commissioning the Apostles, "Go, therefore, and make disciples of all nations, baptizing them in the name of the Father, and of the Son, and of the holy Spirit, teaching them to observe all that I have commanded you" (Matthew 28:19–20). This Great Commission is the primary work of the Church. It is the work of evangelization, the work of inviting all people of all places and times to be friends and disciples of Jesus Christ.

Each time we profess the Nicene-Constantinopolitan Creed at Mass we state, "We believe in one, holy, catholic and apostolic Church." The Church is catholic. She reaches out to all people, as Christ commissioned her to do, and welcomes them into the family of God's Church. The Church is also apostolic. This work is rooted in the commission Jesus first gave to the Apostles. We trace our faith back to the Apostles and the teachings handed on to them by Jesus.

For Reflection

What am I doing or what have I done to "make disciples" for Jesus? What can I do this week to guide the children to tell others that Jesus is their friend?

More Background
For further reading and reflection see *Catechism of the Catholic Church* §§ 748–769, 811–865; *Compendium—Catechism of the Catholic Church* §§ 147–152, 161–176; *United States Catholic Catechism for Adults* pages 16–17, 115–118, 126–136.

About the Children

The spiritual and religious formation of children includes their coming to know and value their identity as members of the Church, the family of God. The child's growing sense of Catholic identity and the development of positive attitudes toward the Church is an important goal of a child's early religious formation. It is vital to the faith development of young children that they find their participation in the local church a welcoming and positive experience. Young children need to experience that they are truly welcomed into the family of believers. Together parents and teachers (and other members of the Church) need to intentionally nurture a sense of belonging in young children.

A Few Suggestions . . .

The things that you do and say in religion class can foster and deepen the children's experience of belonging to the Church. While the Christian home is the primary place threes and fours have their first experiences of belonging to the Church, the religion class builds on and broadens that experience for them. Foster this growing sense of the children's belonging to the Church throughout the year. Involve the children in the celebration of feasts of the Church; visit the church with the children, pointing out the central places, such as the baptismal font, altar, ambo and tabernacle and invite questions. Such experiences help nurture the children's sense of welcome and belonging.

Lesson Planner

Faith Focus

Everyone is welcome to be a friend of Jesus.

Bible Story

"Jesus Makes Two New Friends" (Based on John 1:43–49)

Enriching the Lesson

- RCL Benziger *Stories of God's Love* Music CD and companion Songbook, Song 5
- Visit our preschool Web site www.RCLBenzigerPreschool.com this week.

Chapter Objectives

After this week's lesson the children should be able to:

- recall the Bible story "Jesus Makes Two New Friends."
- discover that the Church is the family of God and is made up of the friends of Jesus.
- thank God for our Church family.

Materials Needed

In addition to the general supplies named on page 9 of this guide, you will need the following materials for teaching this lesson:

- copies of activity master on page 158 of this guide, one for each of the children
- variety of different invitations to share with children as examples
- stickers
- closed Bible with bookmark placed at John 1:43–49

Prayer

Lord God,
you are the Father of all.
Joined to Christ, your Son, in Baptism,
we are your holy people.
Send the Holy Spirit to strengthen us
to proclaim that you invite
all people of every place and time
to become one people in Christ,
the family of your people.
Amen.

17 Jesus Has Many Friends

Stories of God's Love
Ages 3 and 4

Jesus Makes Two New Friends

One day Jesus was walking near where Peter, Andrew, James and John lived. Jesus saw a man named Philip. Philip came from the same city where Peter and Andrew lived.

Jesus said to Philip, "Come, follow me." Philip left what he was doing. He became a friend and follower of Jesus. He would help Jesus do the special work God sent Jesus to do.

Philip then saw a friend of his named Nathanael. He couldn't wait to tell Nathanael about Jesus. He wanted Nathanael to be a friend of Jesus too.

Philip said to Nathanael, "Peter, Andrew and I have found the one who God promised to send us. His name is Jesus. Come with me. I will show him to you." They hurried off to find Jesus.

Seeing Philip and Nathanael, Jesus said, "I know you, Nathanael. You are a very honest man." Nathanael listened to everything Jesus said and became one of the Apostles of Jesus. The Apostles were Jesus' very special friends. Nathanael joined with Peter, Andrew, James, John and Philip to help Jesus do the work God sent him to do.

BASED ON JOHN 1:43–49

 Welcome

- Provide copies of the activity master of the invitation found on page 158 of this guide with the date, time and location already filled in, one for each of the children; a variety of invitations, such as invitations to a birthday party; and stickers to decorate the invitations.
- Greet the children by name and direct them to the Welcome Center. Show them examples of invitations and explain what an invitation is. Relate the purpose of the invitation to the words of Jesus' invitation to Peter, Andrew, James and John in chapter 15, "Friends of Jesus," saying, "An invitation invites us to come somewhere. An invitation to a birthday party invites us to come to a birthday party."
- Tell the children they are going to make an invitation they can give to a friend or family member asking them to come and visit their religion class. Hand out a copy of the activity sheet to each of the children and read the words on the invitation to them.
- Ask the children to decorate their invitation to come visit the religion class. Help them write their name on the invitation. Have them tell you who they want to give their invitation to, and write or help them write that name on the invitation.
- Collect the finished invitations and give the children their invitations to take home at the end of religion class.

 Gather

- Play the gathering song to signal that it is time for the children to clean up and move to the Story Time Area.
- Lead the children in singing song 5 for unit 4 on the *Stories of God's Love* Music CD. Or lead them in singing the song that you selected for unit 4 if you are not using the *Stories of God's Love* Music CD and companion Songbook.

 Teach

Introduce the Bible story.

Show the children the teaching poster or the cover of the children's leaflet for chapter 17. Tell the children that today's lesson is about two very special friends of Jesus. Point to Philip and Nathanael in the illustration. Without telling the children the names of Philip and Nathanael, invite the children to listen to today's Bible story to discover the names of two people Jesus invited to be his very special friends.

Tell the Bible story.

- Invite a child to come up and open the Bible to the place marked by the bookmark, John 1:43–49.
- Take the opened Bible, place the children's leaflet inside. Tell the children the name of the Bible story "Jesus Makes Two New Friends." Refer to the teaching poster or the cover of the children's leaflet as you read the Bible story on the For My Family Page to the children.

Recall the Bible story.

- Help the children recall the key details of today's Bible story by inviting them to respond to these or similar questions.
  - —What were the names of the two new friends of Jesus? *(Philip and Nathanael)* Note: The children will need help in pronouncing these names. Accept appropriate sounding answers and help the children echo the proper pronunciation of the names after you.
  - —What did Jesus say to Philip? *(Come, follow me.)*
  - —Who brought Nathanael to Jesus? *(Philip)*
  - —What did Nathanael do? *(He followed Jesus. He became one of the very special friends of Jesus.)*
- Summarize by telling the children that Philip and Nathanael became very special friends and Apostles of Jesus. They helped Jesus do the work God sent him to do.

 Apply

Work on the children's leaflet activity.

- Ask several children to help you hand out the children's leaflet for chapter 17. Have all the children briefly look at the cover of the leaflet and help them remember the Bible story about Philip and Nathanael.
- Ask the children to open the leaflet to the activity pages. Call their attention to the center image. Point to and read the title "The Friends of Jesus" aloud to the children. Ask them to echo the words of the title after you.
- Invite the children to complete the activity. When all the children have finished tracing and coloring, tell them that the word *Church* is another name for the friends of Jesus. The friends of Jesus come together to pray, to listen to the Bible and to thank God the Father for making us friends of Jesus, his Son. Say the word *Church* aloud and ask them to echo it after you again.
- Summarize by telling the children that the word *Church* is a very special word. Share with them that the Church is the family of God. The name Church is another name for all the friends of Jesus. Emphasize that Jesus wants everyone to be his friend.

Connect with the child's life.

- Ask the children, "Who are some of the people you see when you go to Mass with your family?" Be sure to name the priest if the children do not name the priest as one of the people they see. Note: Be aware that the children's attendance at Mass may vary from child to child. Help the children by asking, "Who remembers seeing the priest?" and so on.
- Hand out the invitations that the children made and tell them to give their invitation to the person they made the invitation for.
- Remind the children to take their leaflet home and share the Bible story on the For My Family Page about Philip and Nathanael and the activity with their family.

Pray

- Gather the children around the prayer table.
- Invite the children to echo the prayer, "Jesus, we are happy to be your friends," after you.
- Call them to a moment of silence. *(Pause.)* Lead the children in prayer. Begin with the Sign of the Cross.

> **Teacher:** God our Father, we belong to your family, the Church. Thank you for our Church family. Jesus, we are happy to be your friends.
> **Children:** *Echo the prayer response,* "Jesus, we are . . ."
> **Teacher:** Together let us pray, "Amen."
> **All:** Amen.

- Conclude by singing with the children the song for unit 4 on the *Stories of God's Love* Music CD or another appropriate song about the Church.

Additional Activity

Play the game "Come, Follow Me."

Use this activity to reinforce the concept of welcoming others.

- Have the children form a circle and sit on the floor. Tell the children they are going to play the game "Come, Follow Me."
- Teach the children to sing these words to the tune of "London Bridge."
  Jesus said, "Come, follow me, follow me, follow me."
  Jesus said, "Come, follow me. I want you as my friend."
- Explain and demonstrate the directions. Invite one child to follow you as you march around the circle. Say, "[Child's name], I invite you to come and follow me." March a small distance around the circle, then invite another child to come join the march and follow you.
- Play the game with the children and continue until all the children are following you.
- Return with the children after making a few passes around the room. Summarize by telling the children how happy we are to have a Church family whose members are all friends of Jesus.

CHAPTER 18

My Church Friends

Background
for the Catechist

The People of God

Through Baptism we are first joined to Christ and receive the gift of the Holy Spirit. At Baptism we receive new life in Jesus Christ and become adopted sons and daughters of God the Father. We become members of the Body of Christ, a larger family of faith, the Church. The Church is the People of God whom God the Father calls together in Christ by the power of the Holy Spirit.

The origin of the Church lies deep within the plan of God from the very beginning of time. It was the design of God in creation to share his own divine life with those he created and to call together all those who believe in Christ in a holy Church. It is God's plan that all people belong to the Church, the new People of God. The Church is the sign and instrument of Salvation. It is the sign and instrument of our reconciliation and communion with God and with one another.

For Reflection

How can my family be a sign that reminds others that God calls all people to be one family, the People of God? What can I do this week to show the children that God wants them all to be friends of Jesus?

More Background

For further reading and reflection see *Catechism of the Catholic Church* §§ 748–786, *Compendium—Catechism of the Catholic Church* §§ 147–155, *United States Catholic Catechism* for Adults pages 111–123.

About the Children

Young children tend to be active, which often means noisy. These natural tendencies of young people can be a challenge for parents and teachers, especially in settings and situations, such as church, where relative quiet and stillness are the expected behaviors. Young children also thrive on predictability. By creating an environment in which children can predict behaviors that are expected of them, you can help children successfully transition from active/noisy to still/quiet behaviors. This experience of success will also help the children enjoy those situations.

A Few Suggestions . . .

Children have the ability to be quiet and still. A preschooler's natural sense of wonder and awe calls forth the response of quiet and stillness. Foster the development of this ability to help the children develop "church skills." Include activities that foster silent and quiet play. Begin and end classroom prayer with a moment of silence. Visit the church with the children and point out that in church there is a time for quiet and listening, a time for praying and singing aloud, a time for sitting and a time for moving. Take time and have the children quietly pray before the Blessed Sacrament with you. Help the children recognize and respond appropriately to these different moments.

Lesson Planner

Faith Focus

My Church friends and I are all friends of Jesus. We all make up our Church family.

Story

"Carlos' Church Friends"

Materials Needed

In addition to the general supplies named on page 9 of this guide, you will need the following materials for teaching this lesson:

- copies of activity masters on pages 159 and 160 of this guide, one for each of the children
- punch-out figures of Carlos, Kim and Abby

Enriching the Lesson

- RCL Benziger *Stories of God's Love* Music CD and companion Songbook, Song 5
- Visit our preschool Web site www.RCLBenzigerPreschool.com this week.

Chapter Objectives

After this week's lesson the children should be able to:

- recall the story "Carlos' Church Friends."
- discover that they have many Church friends who help them come to know God's love for them.
- thank God for all their Church friends.

Prayer

Lord Jesus,
through the Sacrament of Baptism,
I became a member of your Body,
the Church, the People of God.
As I am nourished by the Eucharist,
help me nourish others
with the stories of your life
and the teachings of your Church.
Amen.

Carlos' Church Friends

Carlos looked around the parking lot of the church. He saw his friend Kim from religion class and couldn't wait to get out of the car. Carlos waved, but he wanted to go over to her and say hi.

"Mom, Dad, hurry. I want to get out of the car. I see my friend Kim," said Carlos.

"We are hurrying, honey," Mom answered. "As soon as Daddy parks the car, we'll get out and go see Kim."

Then Carlos saw Abby and her mom. "Look!" shouted Carlos. "Look over there, Mom. There's Abby, my other friend from religion class. She is with her Mom. Hurry, Dad."

Dad parked the car and Mom helped Carlos unbuckle his seat belt. Sliding out of his car seat, Carlos grabbed Mom's hand, saying, "Let's go, Mom and Dad. Hurry. I want to catch Abby and Kim." Carlos pulled on Mom's hand and he, Mom and Dad walked quickly toward Abby and Kim.

"Hi," said Carlos. "Look at my new shoes. I just got them yesterday."

Kim and Abby looked at his new shoes. "I like them," said Kim.

"I like them too," said Abby. "Are you going to church?"

"Yes," answered Carlos. "Hey, Mom and Dad, can we walk into church with my friends, Kim and Abby?"

"I think that would be a great idea," Mom answered. "We are friends with Jesus and friends with each other. I think that is just perfect. Let's go."

Carlos, Abby, Kim and their families all walked into church together. "Good morning," the family at the door greeted them. "Welcome to Holy Spirit Catholic Church. We're glad you are here with us today."

Welcome

- Provide crayons, markers and copies of the activity master found on page 159 of this guide, one for each of the children.
- Greet the children by name and direct them to the Welcome Center. Recall with them the word *church,* which they learned in chapter 16. Hand out the activity sheet to the children. Ask them to look at the pictures around the drawing of the church and explain to them that they can see some of these things in the church and some of these things do not belong in the church. Tell them to find the pictures of things that belong in the church and draw a line from each of those pictures to the picture of the church. Tell them to circle the picture of the thing that does not belong in the church.
- Walk among the children as they are working and help those children who need help. Note: Some threes and young fours may not attend church with their families on a regular basis. These children may have more difficulty with this activity than those children who attend church more regularly.
- Summarize by reviewing the activity. Show the children an activity sheet that you have completed. Name those things that they will see in a church.

Gather

- Play the gathering song to signal that it is time for the children to clean up and move to the Story Time Area.
- Lead the children in singing song 5 for unit 4 on the *Stories of God's Love* Music CD. Or lead the children in singing the song that you selected for unit 4 if you are not using the *Stories of God's Love* Music CD and companion Songbook.

Teach

Introduce the story.

- Show the children the teaching poster or the cover of the children's leaflet for chapter 18. Point to and read the title "My Church Friends" aloud to the children.
- Invite the children to listen to today's story "Carlos' Church Friends" and discover who Carlos saw when he went to church with his parents.

Tell the story.

Tell the children the name of today's story "Carlos' Church Friends." Refer to the teaching poster or the cover of the children's leaflet as you read the story to the children.

Recall the story.

- Provide punch-out figures of Carlos, Kim and Abby.
- Remind the children of the story about the remembering game Jamal played with his parents and how it helped them remember what they saw and heard in church. Tell the children that you will play a remembering game with them today. Ask the children which

punch-out figure they wish to use to help you remember the story. Hand out the figures to the children.

- Explain to the children that you will tell them things you remember about today's story "Carlos' Church Friends." Ask them to raise their figures in the air if they remember the same thing about the story.
  —Carlos, Abby and Kim are friends in religion class. *(Yes.)*
  —Carlos, Abby and Kim were going to church with their families. *(Yes.)*
  —Carlos, Abby and Kim are Church friends too. *(Yes.)*
  —Carlos and his Church friends walk into church together. *(Yes.)*

- Summarize by telling the children, "The Church is the family of God. We have many Church friends. We are all friends of Jesus."

 ## Apply

Work on the children's leaflet activity.

- Ask several children to assist you in handing out the children's leaflet for chapter 18. Have all the children look at the cover of the leaflet to help them recall that Carlos and his friends are going to church with their parents.

- Provide glue or paste and a set of shapes in which are pictures of people you see in church, one for each of the children, made from copies of the activity master on page 160 of this guide.

- Invite the children to open up their leaflet to the activity pages and look at the shapes outlined on the pages. Hand out a set of the shapes containing pictures of people you see in church to each of the children.

- Hold up one shape, name and talk about the people (priest or reader or assembly) in the picture. Have the children match the shape to the appropriate shape on the activity and place it on that shape. Do the same for the remaining pictures.

- Help the children glue or paste the shapes on the activity pages. As you are helping the children share with them that the Church is the family of God and the friends of Jesus. We come together on Sundays and special Holy Days to take part in the celebration of Mass.

My Church Family

Paste the pictures in their shape.
Color the pictures.

Connect with the child's life.

- Ask the children, "Who are some of the people you see at church?" Add responses to the children's answers to reinforce or extend their learning.

- Remind the children to take their leaflet home and share the story on the For My Family Page and the activity with their family.

 ## Pray

- Gather the children around the prayer table.

Teacher:	Let us thank God for giving us our Church family. God our Father, thank you for our Church. We thank you, God.
Children:	*Echo the prayer* "We thank you, God."
Teacher:	Jesus, the Son of God, thank you for our Church. We thank you, God.
Children:	*Echo the prayer* "We thank you, God."
Teacher:	Thank you for Father *(Name),* our pastor. We thank you, God.
Children:	*Echo the prayer* "We thank you, God."
Teacher:	Holy Spirit, thank you for our Church. We thank you, God.
Children:	*Echo the prayer* "We thank you, God."
Teacher:	Together let us pray, "Amen."
All:	Amen.

Additional Activity

Name Church sounds and Church people.

Use this activity to help the children identify the different sounds they might hear at church.

- Provide a small table with two or three chairs. Also provide a tape player containing a collection of sounds the children would hear at church, such as the priest leading prayer, reader reading Scripture and choir singing. Be sure to include a pause between each sound.

- Gather the children and have them sit around you. Show them the recorder and tell them that you will play some of the sounds that they hear in church. Explain to them that you will play the sounds one at a time and they are to tell you the sound and who is making the sound.

- Play the first sound and stop the recorder. Invite the children to listen to and identify the sounds and the person (or people) who is making it. (Option: If you are not able to record church sounds, show the children pictures of a choir, an organist, the priest leading prayer and a reader at a lectern.)

- Invite the children to talk about what each of the people in the pictures does at church.

David Talked with God

Background
for the Catechist

David, Model of Prayer

Sacred Scripture portrays many people who are models of prayer for Christians. David, the shepherd boy who became a king, is one of the Old Testament people who exemplifies what it means to be a person of prayer. From David we learn the primary forms of prayer that the Church uses to express prayers: of blessing and adoration, of petition, of intercession, of thanksgiving and of praise.

David acknowledges God alone to be God and that he is in service of God and the people of God at the invitation of God. David prays both for himself and for others. He acknowledges his weakness and his reliance on God. He turns to God in repentance and sorrow when he sins against God and the people of God. He praises and gives thanks to God whom he acknowledges in trust as the source of all that is good.

For Reflection

What is my favorite form or forms of prayer? Why? What can I do to help the children develop the habit of prayer?

About the Children

The use of language is an important dimension of prayer. Three- and young four-year-olds are growing in their ability to use language. They should be able to name most familiar objects. When they do not know the name of something and ask, "What's this?" teachers and parents have the opportunity to help young children expand their vocabularies. If a child points to a car and says, "My car," you might answer, "Yes, that is your *silver* car. Look how *shiny* it is." If a child is helping you arrange flowers, take the time to describe the flowers, saying, "This is a beautiful white and yellow *daisy.*"

A Few Suggestions . . .

Children also need help in developing the language to name and express concepts that are more abstract. Help them use words to describe things and ideas that they cannot see or touch. For example, when a child is trying to describe feelings, such as fear or joy, help the child begin to label their feelings and express their thoughts about the situations that caused the feelings. These efforts will help the children develop language that will not only assist in the development of their emotional and social skills but also in the ability to express their feelings in prayer.

More Background

For further reading and reflection see *Catechism of the Catholic Church* §§ 2558–2565, 2578–2580, 2626–2643; *Compendium— Catechism of the Catholic Church* §§ 534–535, 538, 550–556; *United States Catholic Catechism for Adults* pages 461–468.

Lesson Planner

Faith Focus

God chose David the shepherd boy to be his good friend. David talked and listened to God in prayer.

Bible Story

"God's Good Friend David" (Based on 1 Samuel 16:11–12, 18; Psalm 5:3; Psalm 17:6)

Enriching the Lesson

- RCL Benziger *Stories of God's Love* Music CD and companion Songbook, Song 6
- Visit our preschool Web site www.RCLBenzigerPreschool.com this week.

Chapter Objectives

After this week's lesson the children should be able to:

- recall the Bible story "God's Good Friend David."
- discover that they can pray anytime.
- thank God for all good things.

Materials Needed

In addition to the general supplies named on page 9 of this guide, you will need the following materials for teaching this lesson:

- white paper with word *Pray* written in white crayon on each piece of paper, one for each of the children
- dark, thinned watercolor paints; brushes
- small cups of water, towels
- closed Bible with bookmark at 1 Samuel 16:11

Prayer

Lord God,
send the Holy Spirit
to teach me to pray.
Strengthen and deepen
my communion with you in prayer.
Guide me to be a model of prayer
for the children in my care.
Amen.

19 David Talked with God

Stories of God's Love — Ages 3 and 4

God's Good Friend David

In the Bible we read about a young boy named David. David was a shepherd who watched over his family's sheep. He loved God very much. God loved David too and chose him to become the king of many people.

When he was a shepherd and when he was king, David prayed often to God. He prayed to God when he was happy and he prayed to God when he was sad. He prayed to God when he was joyful and he prayed to God when he was frightened. David prayed to tell God how much he loved him. He prayed just to tell God how wonderful and good he is.

Whatever David did or wherever David went, he always remembered to pray. He talked to God every day. He thanked God for all the good things God gave to him and asked God to help him do what he should do each day.

Many of David's prayers are in the Bible.

BASED ON 1 SAMUEL 16:11-12, 18; PSALM 5:3; PSALM 17:6

 Welcome

- Provide sheets of white paper on which you have written the word *Pray* using a white crayon, one sheet of paper for each of the children; dark, thinned watercolor paints; paintbrushes and small cups of water.
- Greet the children by name and direct them to the Welcome Center. Show the children the paper and tell them there is a secret message on the paper. Explain to them that they will use the paint to discover the secret message.
- Demonstrate for the children how to dip their brush in the watercolor paint, tap the brush on the side of the paint container to eliminate the excess paint and then lightly brush the paint over the paper to discover the hidden word.
- Have the children do the activity.
- Show the children a sheet that you have completed and point to and read the word *Pray* aloud to the children after the children have completed the activity. Invite the children to echo the word after you.
- Tell the children that when we pray we listen and talk to God. We share with God what we are feeling and what we are thinking.

 Gather

- Play the gathering song to signal that it is time for the children to clean up and move to the Story Time Area.
- Assist the children in laying their papers in a place to dry. Make sure to write the child's name or help the child write their name on their paper.
- Introduce song 6 for unit 5 on the *Stories of God's Love* Music CD to the children. Or introduce the children to another appropriate song about prayer that they will sing during unit 5 (chapters 19, 20, 21 and 22) if you are not using the *Stories of God's Love* Music CD and its companion Songbook.

 Teach

Introduce the Bible story.

- Show the children the teaching poster or the cover of the children's leaflet for chapter 19. Tell them that today's lesson is about a friend of God named David who showed us how to pray. Remind the children that we pray when we talk and listen to God.
- Tell the children David lived a long time ago, and invite them to listen to a Bible story to discover how David prayed.

Tell the Bible story.

- Invite one of the children to come up and open the Bible to the page marked by the bookmark at 1 Samuel 16:11.
- Take the opened Bible, place the children's leaflet inside. Tell the children the name of the Bible story "God's Good Friend David." Refer to the teaching poster or the cover of

the children's leaflet as you read the Bible story on the For My Family Page to the children.

Recall the Bible story.

- Invite the children to play a rhythm game to help them recall the details of the Bible story "God's Good Friend David." Instruct them to sit with their legs stretched out in front of them and echo the words and imitate the motions of the game after you. Use both hands to tap on your legs when you say each word:

    David was a shepherd boy. / Then he was a king.
    He prayed to God / every day. / He loved to pray and sing.

- Summarize by reminding the children that David showed that he was God's friend when he prayed.

 ## Apply

Work on the children's leaflet activity.

- Have several children help you hand out the children's leaflet for chapter 19. Ask everyone to briefly look at the cover and then open their leaflet. Read the title on the activity page to the children.
- Invite the children to complete the dot-to-dot activity to discover different places and times that they can talk and listen to God.
- Walk among the children and help those children who need assistance in doing the activity. Ask them to tell you what they see in each completed picture when all the children have completed the activity.
- Call the children's attention to each of the pictures and encourage them to think of something that they might pray about at these different places and times.
- Summarize by telling the children that we can pray anywhere and anytime just as David did.

Connect with the child's life.

- Ask the children to tell you one thing that they can talk to God about today. Say, "That is a wonderful thing to share with God" after each child responds.
- Remind the children to take their leaflet home and to share the Bible story and activity with their family.

Talking and Listening to God

Connect the dots.
Discover when and where you can pray.
Tell a friend when you will pray.

- Hand out the "Pray" activity sheets that the children completed at the beginning of the lesson. Tell them to take them home and to put them near their beds. Explain that this will help them remember to pray every night before they go to sleep.

 ## Pray

- Gather the children at the prayer table.
- Explain that in today's prayer they will pray quietly in their hearts. Tell them that you will begin the prayer. Next they will pray quietly in their hearts telling God anything they want to share with him.
- Call the children to pray by having them repeat after you: "My head I bow. / My hands I fold. / Now I talk to God." *(Pause.)*
- Lead the children in prayer. Begin with the Sign of the Cross.

    Teacher: Come, Holy Spirit. Help us to pray. We now pray to you quietly in our hearts. *(Pause.)*
    Children: *Children pray quietly in their hearts.*
    Teacher: Thank you for listening to our prayers. We love you with all our heart.
    All: Amen.

Additional Activity

Learn a song of prayer.
Use this activity to reinforce the concept that we can pray at different times and in different ways.

- Remind the children that David prayed every day. Explain to them that we can pray every day too. Tell them that you will teach them the words and motions to a song about praying, and then you will sing it together.
- Teach the children these lyrics to the tune of "She'll Be Coming 'Round the Mountain." Use these motions: For verse one, place hands together in prayer, then nod head yes. For verse two, place hand around ear, then nod head yes.

    I can pray every morning, yes I can.
    I can pray every morning, yes I can.
    I can pray every morning, I can pray every morning,
    I can pray every morning, yes I can.

    God hears me every morning, yes he does.
    God hears me every morning, yes he does.
    God hears me every morning, God hears me every
        morning,
    God hears me every morning, yes he does.

- Sing the song a second time, substituting the word *nighttime* for the word *morning*.

I Pray Every Day

Background
for the Catechist

Pray Without Ceasing
Always Give Thanks

Paul the Apostle exhorts us to live, to rejoice in the love of God revealed in Jesus Christ. "Rejoice always. Pray without ceasing. In all circumstances give thanks, for this is the will of God for you in Christ Jesus" (1 Thessalonians 5:16–18).

Christians are a "thanksgiving" people. The greatest prayer of the Church, the Eucharist, is a prayer of praise and thanksgiving. In this prayer, the Church is joined to Christ and gives thanks to God the Father through the power of the Holy Spirit for his loving deeds of creation and Salvation.

Every moment and occasion in our daily lives is a time for prayer, for sharing our thoughts and feelings with God. It is sometimes easier to raise our heart and voice in thanks to the Lord in good times when we feel blessed. But both blessings and needs can be an offering of thanksgiving. The love of family, friends and neighbors, who celebrate with us in times of joy and comfort us in times of suffering, reminds us that God's sustaining love always surrounds us.

For Reflection

When do I stop, place myself in the presence of God and pray each day? In what ways do I integrate prayer into my time with the children other than those called for by the lesson plan?

About the Children

All human beings—children, youth and adults—need to feel that they have the ability and "power" to make decisions. Young children need to be guided and empowered to make appropriate choices. They need to be given opportunities to practice this skill and experience the consequences of making choices. Providing children with such opportunities will help them develop the foundation for making more complex decisions. It will help lay the foundation for their growth as responsible persons.

A Few Suggestions . . .

Provide the children with small opportunities to make a few simple decisions each day. These decisions could include praying every day, choosing what activities they want to participate in, what color marker or markers to use, whether to use crayons or markers, glue or paste. Encourage them to make choices and be patient with the children's choices. Help the children identify the consequences of both good and bad choices. Give positive feedback to choices that show respect for the other children and for you.

More Background

For further reading and reflection see *Catechism of the Catholic Church* §§ 2637–2638, 2659–2660, 2663–2672; *Compendium— Catechism of the Catholic Church* §§ 555, 558, 559– 561; *United States Catholic Catechism for Adults* pages 466–468, 476–477.

Lesson Planner

Faith Focus

We pray every day. We thank God for all he has given us.

Story

"Abby Says 'Thank You' to God"

Materials Needed

In addition to the general supplies named on page 9 of this guide, you will need the following materials for teaching this lesson:

- copies of activity master on page 161 of this guide, one for each of the children

Enriching the Lesson

- RCL Benziger *Stories of God's Love* Music CD and companion Songbook, Song 6
- Visit our preschool Web site www.RCLBenzigerPreschool.com this week.

Chapter Objectives

After this week's lesson the children should be able to:

- recall the story "Abby Says 'Thank You' to God."
- discover things they want to thank God for.
- thank God for all he has given them.

Prayer

God our Father,
I recognize the many blessings in my life
and come to you with a thankful heart.
Send the Holy Spirit
to help me teach the children
to see that you have given them many gifts
and to take time to thank you for those gifts.
Amen.

Abby Says "Thank You" to God

Every night when Mom came to Abby's room at bedtime, Abby knew it was time for her to say her prayers. Abby said her nighttime prayers every night before she went to sleep. It was a special time for her and her mom.

"Abby, what are we going to pray for tonight?" asked Mom as she knelt next to Abby and the dolls Abby had lined up on the floor next to her bed.

"Tonight, I want to say thank you to God," Abby answered her mom.

"What a wonderful thing to do, Abby. God loves it when we pray and say thank you to him. What would you like to thank God for tonight?" Mom asked.

Abby bowed her head, closed her eyes, and said, "Hi, God. This is Abby." She continued, "Thank you for my mommy. She is really fun, and she takes good care of me every day. She cooks good too. Thank you for my grandma and grandpa. I love them a whole bunch. Thank you also for all my toys, especially my dolls. I have lots of fun with them. Thanks for all those things, and good night to you too. Amen."

"That was a beautiful prayer, Sweetie," Mom said. "We have so many things to be thankful for, don't we? Now I want to say a special thank you to God."

"Thank you, God, for Abby. I love her so much," Mom prayed and gave Abby a hug.

"Isn't it wonderful that God hears our words and our thoughts?" Mom said. "Now let's get all snuggled in bed for our story."

 Welcome

- Provide the pictures of the praying children that you have made from the activity master found on page 161 of this guide, one copy for each of the children.
- Greet the children by name and direct them to the Welcome Center.
- Give each of the children a copy of the activity master. Invite the children to color the pictures.
- Walk among the children as they are working. Remind them to pray each day and thank God for the people who love and care for them and for the many other blessings that God has given them.
- Tell the children to bring their colored pictures to the Story Time Area.

 Gather

- Play the gathering song to signal that it is time for the children to clean up and move to the Story Time Area. Have the children bring their colored pictures with them.
- Lead the children in singing song 6 for unit 5 on the *Stories of God's Love* Music CD. Or lead the children in singing the song you selected for unit 5 if you are not using the *Stories of God's Love* Music CD and its companion Songbook.
- Have the children hold their own hands together to make praying hands. Ask them to think about someone they want to pray for and thank God for that person and ask God to bless that person.

 Teach

Introduce the story.

- Show the children the teaching poster or the cover of the children's leaflet for this chapter. Point to and read aloud the title "I Pray Every Day."
- Call attention to Abby in the illustration. Tell the children to listen carefully to today's story to discover what Abby said to God in her bedtime prayer.

Tell the story.

Tell the children the name of the story "Abby Says 'Thank You' to God." Refer to the teaching poster or the cover of the children's leaflet as you read the story to the children.

Recall the story.

- Help the children recall details from the story. Tell them that you will name some of the things Abby thanked God for. Ask them to hold up the pictures of the praying children that they colored if you name something that Abby thanked God for in her bedtime prayer. Name the items, pausing after each so the children can hold up their colored pictures.

her mom *(Yes)*	her grandpa *(Yes)*
her grandma *(Yes)*	her toys *(Yes)*
apples and oranges *(No)*	

- Conclude by telling the children that saying thank you is very important. It is especially important for them to say thank you to God who loves them and everyone so much.

Apply

Work on the children's leaflet activity.

- Ask several children to help you hand out the children's leaflet for this chapter. Have the children look at the cover to briefly recall today's story "Abby Says 'Thank You' to God."
- Ask the children to open their leaflet and call their attention to the four pictures on the pages. Ask volunteers to name the time of the day that each picture tells about.
- Name the time of the day the top left picture identifies. *(The morning)* Tell the children, "Color the cross next to the picture if you can pray in the morning."
- Repeat the process for the remaining three pictures.
- Congratulate the children for their responses.

Connect with the child's life.

- Remind the children that in her bedtime prayer Abby thanked God for many people and things. Ask:
    - —Who will you thank God for tonight at bedtime?
    - —What things will you thank God for tonight at bedtime?
- Remind the children to take home their leaflet and share the story on the For My Family Page and the activity with their families. Also remind them to take home the picture that they colored.

Pray

- Gather the children at the prayer table.
- Show the children the pictures of the children praying and remind them that prayer is listening and talking to God. Explain to the children that you will lead them in singing a prayer today that gives thanks to God.
- Explain that they will sing the words of the prayer to the tune of "If You're Happy and You Know It." Tell them that they can name something or someone they want to thank God for when you pause *(demonstrate by singing the first line of the song)*. Optional: Have the children begin by holding their

hands together in the traditional prayer gesture and opening and clapping their hands when they pray "yes, we do."

- Practice singing the prayer with the children:
    Oh, we thank you, God, for *(pause)*, yes, we do.
    Oh, we thank you, God, for *(pause)*, yes, we do.
    When we stop to think and pray,
    we thank you every day.
    Oh, we thank you, God, for *(pause)*, yes, we do.
- Call the children to a moment of silence. *(Pause.)* Lead them in prayer. Begin with the Sign of the Cross.

Additional Activities

Create and display a "Thank-You God" chart.
Use this activity to reinforce the concept that one way to pray is to thank God for the many good things in our life.
- Provide a chart with the heading "Thank You, God, for Making _____!" Write this or another list under the heading:
    People Who Smile   Things That Are Small
    Things That Are Round   Things That Are Soft
- Display the chart where every child can easily see it. Call the children's attention to the chart. Read the heading and tell them that there are many people and things we thank God for each day as Abby did. Read the first item on the list and give examples. Write or draw the things they name on the chart. Continue the activity until the chart is completed.
- Conclude by telling the children that there are many other people and things we can thank God for each day.
- Display the chart in the Prayer Area or at the entrance to the learning area as a reminder for the children to thank God for the people who love and care for them and for the many other blessings they have received from God.

Make a class prayer box.
Use this activity to help the children remember to pray prayers of thanksgiving.
- Provide a shoe box and a lid covered with plain paper with the words "Our Prayers" written on the lid. You might want to decorate the prayer box. This will create and foster interest among the children.
- Show the prayer box to the children. Tell them that when they have something that they would like to pray for, they can draw a picture of it or have a teacher write it down, and they can put the picture or note in the box. Explain that when the class prays each day, everyone will pray for everything that is in the box.

I Love You, God!

Tell what time of the day it is in each picture.
Color the crosses when you pray.

CHAPTER 21

David Sang His Prayers

Background
for the Catechist

The Prayer of Christians

Prayer is an invitation from God. It is a primary means of expressing and deepening our relationship with God who is continuously inviting us to live in communion and covenant with him. Transformed by the love of God, we long to respond to that love. Through prayer we share our thoughts and feelings, our needs and desires, our joys and sorrows with him in whose presence we constantly live.

Christian prayer reflects and is modeled on the prayer of Jesus. In the Christian tradition there are three major expressions of prayer. They are vocal prayer, meditative prayer and contemplative prayer. In vocal prayer we follow the example of Christ who lifted his voice to his Father alone and with others. In the prayer of meditation we, as Christ did, seek to know the Father's will and attune our hearts and minds to what God is asking of us. In the prayer of contemplation we quietly place ourselves in the presence of him we address as "Abba," conversing with him in childlike trust.

For Reflection

What is my preferred way to pray? Why? What can I do to help the children experience the different kinds of prayer?

About the Children

Music and movement activities help young children become actively involved in their learning. Music relates to young children's need to move and be engaged in their environment. While the children are joyfully engaged in such activities, important learning takes place. Music develops listening skills and auditory awareness, contributes to speech and language development and encourages creativity.

A Few Suggestions . . .

Add music and movement to activities. Children are drawn into an activity that is supported by music and movement. Check hymns your parish regularly sings. Teach the children the chorus of hymns that young children can easily join with the assembly in singing. Choose songs that have easy-to-learn phrases. Repeat the singing of songs. Learning a song takes time, so repetition is very important. When young children sing a song over and over, they can become familiar and comfortable with it. This increases the child's ability to enjoy singing it with the group. Join in the singing of the songs. If you are uncomfortable singing, don't worry. Children rarely notice the quality of the teacher's voice. What they do notice is that you are enjoying singing with them.

More Background

For further reading and reflection see *Catechism of the Catholic Church* §§ 2650–2651, 2663–2673, 2697–2719; *Compendium— Catechism of the Catholic Church* §§ 557, 559, 567– 571; *United States Catholic Catechism for Adults* pages 473–477.

Lesson Planner

Faith Focus

David sang his prayers.

Bible Story

"David Sang His Prayers" (Based on 1 Samuel 16:11b–12, 16:18; 2 Samuel 5:4–5; Psalm 23; Psalm 25)

Enriching the Lesson

- RCL Benziger *Stories of God's Love* Music CD and companion Songbook, Song 6
- Visit our preschool Web site www.RCLBenzigerPreschool.com this week.

Chapter Objectives

After this week's lesson the children should be able to:

- recall the Bible story "David Sang His Prayers."
- discover that they can speak and sing their prayers to God.
- thank God in a song for all he has given them.

Materials Needed

In addition to the general supplies named on page 9 of this guide, you will need the following materials for teaching this lesson:

- pieces of white paper, one for each of the children
- crayons, glitter, glue, stickers
- closed Bible with bookmark placed at Psalm 23

Prayer

Thank you, God,
for the gift of prayer.
Help me sing your praises
through everything I do.
Guide me to teach the children
to lift their voices in praise of you.
Amen.

21 David Sang His Prayers

Stories of God's Love
Ages 3 and 4

David Sang His Prayers

When David was a young boy, he was a shepherd and he helped take care of his family's sheep. While watching over his family's sheep, David sometimes just sat down and made sure they were safe. He had time to look at the beautiful blue sky, the green grass and the water flowing in the stream. David watched little lambs playing and heard birds singing. Seeing and hearing all these things, David came to know how wonderful and good God is.

The Bible tells us that David often talked to God in prayer. He also sang his prayers to God. He would play music on an instrument called a lyre *(show picture)* and sing prayers of thanks to God for all the things he saw. He sang prayers of thanks for the mountains, for water, for all the animals and for the moon and the sun.

David sang prayers of thanks to God for taking care of him and for helping him do the things that he should. He sang prayers asking God for forgiveness. Many of the prayers David sang are in the Bible.

BASED ON 1 SAMUEL 16:11b–12, 16:18, 2 SAMUEL 5:4–5, PSALM 23, PSALM 25

Welcome

- Provide pieces of plain paper, one for each of the children, folded in half into the shape of a card on the cover of which you have printed "I Am Praying for You"; crayons; markers; glitter and other decorative times, such as stickers.
- Greet the children by name and direct them to the Welcome Center. Give each of the children a "card." Point to and read the words on the cover to them and ask them to echo the words after you. Remind the children what it means to pray. *(To talk with God, to listen to God, to share with God what is on our minds and in our hearts)*
- Explain to the children that they will make a card to give to someone they wish to pray for. Ask them to think of someone they want to pray for. Tell the children to open their cards. Help them write the name of the person on the inside of the card for them.
- Invite the children to decorate the card. Have them begin by decorating the cover, using crayons, markers and any other materials you have supplied.
- Walk among the children and assist the children in writing their name on the inside of the card.
- Collect and put the finished cards in a special place for the children to take home.

Gather

- Play the gathering song to signal that it is time for the children to clean up and move to the Story Time Area.
- Lead the children in singing song 6 for unit 5 on the *Stories of God's Love* Music CD. Or lead the children in singing the song that you selected for unit 5 if you are not using the *Stories of God's Love* Music CD and its companion Songbook.

Teach

Introduce the Bible story.

- Show the children the teaching poster or the cover of the children's leaflet for chapter 19. Point to the illustration of David and ask:
   —Who can tell me the name of the shepherd in the picture? *(David)*
   —Who can tell me about David? *(David was a shepherd. David was God's good friend. David became a king. David prayed a lot.)*
- Next, show the children the teaching poster or the cover of the children's leaflet for chapter 21. Invite the children to listen to another Bible story about God's good friend David to discover a special way David prayed.

Tell the Bible story.

- Invite a child to come up and open the closed Bible to the place marked by the bookmark, Psalm 23.
- Take the opened Bible and place the children's leaflet inside. Tell the children the name of the Bible story "David Sang His Prayers." Refer to the teaching poster or the cover of the children's leaflet as you read the Bible story on the For My Family Page to the children.

Recall the Bible story.

- Help the children recall today's Bible story. Point to the lyre in the illustration. Remind the children of the name of the instrument that David played while he sang his prayers and have the children repeat the word *lyre* after you.
- Tell the children that you will tell them things that you remember about the Bible story. Invite them to wave both hands in the air if what you tell them really happened in the Bible story.
- Read the statements one at a time. Pause after each, allowing the children time to respond.
    - —David was a shepherd. *(True)*
    - —David played music on his piano. *(False)*
    - —David sang a prayer of thanks for the mountains and the moon and the sun. *(True)*
    - —David wrote many songs that were prayers. *(True)*
- Summarize by reminding the children that just like David, we can sing our prayers too.

 Apply

Work on the children's leaflet activity.

- Have several children help you hand out the children's leaflet for chapter 21. Ask everyone to briefly look at the cover. Point to the lyre and say, "This is a lyre. It is the musical instrument David played. Together let us say the word *lyre*."
- Ask the children to open their leaflet. Point to the title on the page "We Sing Our Prayers" and read it to the children. Have the children look at the pictures on the page. Talk with them about each of the pictures and have them color

We Sing Our Prayers

Color your favorite animals.
Sing, "Thank you, God."

the things in creation for which they want to thank God. Invite them to sing "Thank you, God" as they color.

- Conclude by telling the children that we sing our prayers with our Church family every Sunday when we go to church. The songs we sing are called hymns.

Connect with the child's life.

- Ask the children to talk about the things in creation they see and hear. Ask, "Which of these things will you thank God for tonight when you pray your bedtime prayer?"
- Give each of the children their prayer card and encourage them to give it to the person named inside the card.
- Remind the children to take their leaflet home and to share the Bible story on the For My Family Page and the activity with their families.

 Pray

- Gather the children at the prayer table.
- Explain to the children that they will sing their prayer today. Practice singing the prayer for the children, one line at a time, to the tune of "Twinkle, Twinkle, Little Star":
    Thank you, God, my prayers you hear. / Thank you for your love so dear. / Every night and every day. / With my voice and hands I pray. / Thank you, God, my prayers you hear. / Thank you for your love so dear.
- Call the children to a moment of silence. *(Pause.)* Lead them in prayer. Begin with the Sign of the Cross.

Additional Activity

Create musical instruments.

Use this activity to reinforce the concept that we sometimes sing our prayers.

- Provide empty paper-towel or toilet-paper tubes, rubber bands and pieces of wax paper large enough to cover one end of the tube, enough for each of the children.
- Explain to the children that you and they will work together to make musical instruments. Show them the instrument you made in preparation for the lesson.
- Hand out the tubes and invite the children to decorate them. Help the children wrap one end of their tube tightly with wax paper and secure it with a rubber band after they have finished decorating it.
- Take your instrument and show the children how to play it. Invite them to join you in humming into their instruments, which will create a kazoo-like sound.
- Conclude by saying, "How wonderful it is that we can use our voices and music and sing our prayers."

I Can Sing My Prayers

Background
for the Catechist

The Habit of Prayer

Praying is vital to the Christian life. Prayer nurtures our communion and covenant with God. Prayer is both initiated by God and is our response to the invitation of the Holy Spirit who invites, urges, coaches and teaches us to pray.

There is no place we cannot pray. There is no time we cannot pray. We simply need to be aware of the Holy Spirit's presence and invitation. If we make the effort to pause, to be still and silent, to be touched by the Holy Spirit's presence and love, we will pray as naturally as we breathe. The rhythm of praying will become as much a part of our life as the rhythm of breathing.

Prayer and the Christian life are inseparable. Saint Gregory reminded us, "We must remember God more often than we draw breath." That is why we need to cultivate the habit of praying. We develop the habit of praying by making the effort to pray each day in the morning, in the evening, at mealtimes and by regularly joining with our Church family to celebrate the Eucharist on Sundays, on Holy Days of Obligation and on other feasts. While prayer is first an invitation of God, it also always demands effort on our part.

For Reflection

What efforts do I make to grow as a person of prayer? What can I do to guide the children to pray each and every day?

About the Children

Young children experience affection and learn to appropriately express affection from their families. All young children need to feel care and concern from the adults around them. This is important for their emotional growth and it helps them learn how to express warmth and care to others. When they are shown respect, they learn to respect others. When they are appropriately shown love, children learn to appropriately show their love for others. The care and friendliness you have shown to the children this year will help them feel a part of the faith community.

A Few Suggestions . . .

The children in your class look to you as a model for all behavior. By receiving love and respect from you, they will learn to treat each other in the same manner. Most children will respond well to your care and friendliness, yet some may be more reserved. In such situations be predictable and continue to respond with smiles and verbal affirmations. Highlight positive interactions and behaviors in the classroom that show respect for their peers and for others. Such affirmation encourages the children to continue to develop those behaviors.

More Background

For further reading and reflection see *Catechism of the Catholic Church* §§ 2663–2672, 2683–2691, 2725–2745; *Compendium— Catechism of the Catholic Church* §§ 559–561, 565– 566, 572–577; *United States Catholic Catechism for Adults* pages 468–469, 472, 476–477.

Lesson Planner

Faith Focus

We sing songs with our family and friends to tell God that we love him.

Story

"Kim's BIG Surprise"

Enriching the Lesson

- RCL Benziger *Stories of God's Love* Music CD and companion Songbook, Song 6
- Visit our preschool Web site www.RCLBenzigerPreschool.com this week.

Chapter Objectives

After this week's lesson the children should be able to:

- recall the story "Kim's BIG Surprise."
- discover that they can pray with songs and musical instruments.
- thank God with music for his love for them.

Materials Needed

In addition to the general supplies named on page 9 of this guide, you will need the following materials for teaching this lesson:

- empty snack cans with lids
- sound-making objects
- pre-cut sheets of paper, large enough to cover snack cans
- punch-out figure of Kim

Prayer

Lord God, Father of all,
send the Holy Spirit
to teach me to lead the children
to you in prayer.
Help me always listen to the children
in a prayerful way,
for in them I hear your voice.
Amen.

Kim's BIG Surprise

Kim was singing and dancing 'round and 'round. Skipping out of her room into the living room where the whole family was sitting, Kim was singing, "La, la, la, I love to sing. La, la, la, the bells will ring." Grandpa and Grandma were on the couch, Daddy was holding baby Mya and Mommy was reading. Everyone looked up at her when she came in.

"My, my, you sure are a happy girl today," Grandpa said. "Tell us why you are so happy."

Kim danced in a few circles, singing her song, then stopped in the middle of the room and said, "I am so happy because I have a big surprise for you."

"Well, now," Daddy said. "Let's hear all about this BIGGGG surprise."

Filled with excitement, Kim proudly told everyone, "Miss Diaz picked me to play the drums in the big party next Sunday in religion class."

"That's wonderful, Sweetie," said Mommy. "Tell us more about the party."

"We're going to have songs and snacks, and you are all invited to come. We learned a song, but I can't sing it for you now because it's a surprise! Carlos and Abby are going to play the bells, Jamal gets to bang the tambourine and I get to play the drums. I'm really good. I love to play the drums! I can't wait for you to hear us."

"Now we're excited too," Daddy said. "We can't wait to be there. But why are you having this big party?"

"We get to have a party and sing to show Jesus how much we love him. And I can't wait!" said Kim.

"We can't wait to be there with you," said Kim's family.

Welcome

- Provide shakers made from snack-size cans with lids and a selection of sound-making materials. If needed, make enough for half of the children to share. Also provide paper to cover the shakers that they will decorate. Make sure the lids are securely attached to the snack-size cans.
- Greet the children by name and direct them to the Welcome Center. Show the children your shaker and explain to them that they will decorate their own shakers, using the materials you have provided.
- Explain the directions and ask the children to begin decorating their shakers. Walk among the children as they are working and help the children who need assistance.
- Have the children join with you and make music with their shakers. As they are playing their new instruments, tell the children they will use their shakers in the Prayer Center today to give thanks to God. Invite them to place the shakers on a table for now.

Gather

- Play the gathering song to signal that it is time for the children to clean up and move to the Story Time Area.
- Lead the children in singing song 6 for unit 5 on the *Stories of God's Love* Music CD. Or lead the children in singing the song that you have selected for unit 5 if you are not using the *Stories of God's Love* Music CD and its companion Songbook.

Teach

Introduce the story.

- Show the children the teaching poster or the cover of the children's leaflet. Tell the children that today's lesson is about singing our prayers.
- Call the children's attention to Kim and her family on the teaching poster or cover of the children's leaflet. Invite them to listen to the story to discover why Kim was singing and dancing for her family.

Tell the story.

Tell the children the name of today's story "Kim's BIG Surprise." Refer to the teaching poster or the cover of the children's leaflet as you read the story to the children.

I Can Sing My Prayers

Recall the story.

- Help the children recall the story. Tell the children you will ask them four questions about the story you just read to them. Explain that after each question you will hold up your punch-out figure of Kim and invite them to tell you the answer to the question all together. Provide clues as necessary:
  —Who was the story about? *(Kim)*
  —What was Kim doing? *(Singing and dancing)*
  —What was Kim's BIG surprise? *(She gets to play the drums during a party in religion class.)*
  —Why are Kim and her friends having a party during religion class? *(To tell Jesus how much they love him.)*
- Summarize by telling the children that singing songs and playing instruments can help us pray.

 ## Apply

Work on the children's leaflet activity.

- Have several children help you hand out the children's leaflet for chapter 22. Ask everyone to briefly look at the cover and tell you what Kim is doing. *(Kim is dancing and singing because she is very happy.)*
- Ask the children to open their leaflet and ask them to look at the title "Making Music for God" and read it to them. Have the children look at the illustrations. Invite the children to name the musical instruments one at a time. Ask, "Can playing the piano help us pray?" *(Yes)* Then instruct the children to circle the picture of the piano. Repeat the process for all the instruments on the page.
- Conclude by telling the children that we can use songs and musical instruments to pray and show God how much we love him.

Connect with the child's life.

- Tell the children that the world is full of wonderful sounds that remind us of God's love for us. Ask, "What sounds do you hear that remind you of God's love for us?" Give an example of a sound that you hear and tell why it helps you remember God's love. Ask the question again and call

Making Music for God

Circle the instruments that help make music for God.

on volunteers to name sounds they hear that remind them of God's love.

- Remind the children to take their leaflet home and to share the story and the activity with their families.

 ## Pray

- Gather the children at the prayer table and hand out the shakers they made. Remind them that they will use their shakers to make the music for today's prayer. Practice singing the prayer with the children to the tune of "If You're Happy and You Know It." Have them play their shakers at the end of each line after they sing, "yes, we do."
  Oh, we sing our thanks to God, yes, we do.
  Oh, we sing our thanks to God, yes, we do.
  Oh, we love to sing and pray. We thank God every day.
  Oh, we sing our thanks to God, yes, we do.
- Call the children to a moment of silence. *(Pause.)* Lead the children in singing the prayer. Begin with the Sign of the Cross. If time allows, invite them to sing the song again, this time while walking in a procession around the room.
- Tell the children to take their shakers home.

Additional Activity

Use a beanbag to help us pray.
Use this activity to reinforce that we can sing and use music to pray.

- Provide a beanbag, CD player and music.
- Gather the children in a circle on the floor. Explain to the children that you will play a song and that they will pass a beanbag around the circle to one another as the music is playing. Tell them that when the music stops, the child with the beanbag will tell everyone something they want to thank God for. Then everyone in the group will sing a prayer to thank God for what the child named. Create a simple one- or two-note melody and practice singing a prayer with the group, for example, "Johnny is thankful for sunshine."
- Begin the activity. Play song 17, the instrumental version of the song from the *Stories of God's Love* Music CD for unit 5, or play a recording of another appropriate song. Stop the song and ask the child holding the beanbag, "What do you want to thank God for?" Invite everyone to sing a thank-you prayer.
- Play the music again and repeat the process until every child gets an opportunity to say one thing they are thankful for.

CHAPTER 23

All Saints Day

Background
for the Catechist

The Communion of the Saints

The Church is the People of God, a Communion of Saints, a communion of holy people and holy things. Every person is called to a life of holiness. The Holy Spirit is the source of the Church's holiness, her "saintliness." The Holy Spirit dwells within each of the baptized and within the whole Church.

The Communion of Saints includes all the faithful members of the Church on earth and those who have died. It includes both the saints living in communion with God in Heaven and those faithful in Purgatory who are being prepared to receive the gift of eternal life with God.

The saints living in Heaven care about us and for us. They serve the faithful on earth as our intercessors before God in Heaven. This faith moves us to pray to them and to learn about their lives on earth. In this lesson the children will learn about Saint Thérèse of Lisieux, Saint Juan Diego, Saint Elizabeth Ann Seton and Saint Francis of Assisi.

For Reflection

What does it mean to me to live a life of holiness? What can I do to help the children see themselves as holy people?

About the Children

Some stories of saints can help young children come to understand how God wants us to live our lives. By being selective and carefully choosing saints and other people recognized as holy by the Church that young children can relate to, it is possible to explain good deeds in a way that most children can understand. For example, explain that everything Saint Thérèse did, even the little things she did, she did out of her love for God; Saint Juan Diego spent a lot of time learning about Jesus; Saint Elizabeth Ann Seton taught children about God's love for them; and Saint Francis of Assisi was known for his kindness to animals. Saint Martin de Porres cared for the sick and people who were poor.

A Few Suggestions . . .

Engage the children in conversation about the saints. Focus on ways the saints lived as Jesus taught us to do. When possible connect the stories of saints with the Gospel stories about Jesus and his teachings. If any of the children in the class have the names of saints whose lives you are familiar with, talk about those saints. By sharing stories about the saints that young children can relate to, you can plant the seeds of curiosity that will guide their learning in future years.

More Background

For further reading and reflection see *Catechism of the Catholic Church* §§ 823–829, 946–953, 2012–2016; *Compendium—Catechism of the Catholic Church* §§ 165, 194–195, 428; *United States Catholic Catechism for Adults* pages 116–121, 138–139, 195–197.

Lesson Planner

Faith Focus

Saints show us how to love God and live as friends of Jesus.

Story

"Dressing Up as Saints"

Enriching the Lesson

- RCL Benziger *Stories of God's Love* Music CD and companion Songbook, Song 1
- Visit our preschool Web site www.RCLBenzigerPreschool.com this week.

Chapter Objectives

After this week's lesson the children should be able to:

- recall the story "Dressing Up as Saints."
- discover that the saints were God's special helpers.
- thank God for giving them the saints to help them live as friends of Jesus.

Materials Needed

In addition to the general supplies named on page 9 of this guide, you will need the following materials for teaching this lesson:

- copies of activity master on page 162 of this guide, one copy for each of the children

Prayer

Lord God, our Father,
you call us to live holy lives.
Send the Holy Spirit
to fill our hearts with your love.
Strengthen us to love you
with our whole mind, heart and soul
and others as we love ourselves
as Jesus your Son commanded.
Amen.

Dressing Up as Saints

"Come, sit around me in a circle," Miss Diaz asked the children. All the children came quickly and sat on the bright red carpet. Today at religion class the children did not look like themselves. They were dressed up in a special way. It was All Saints Day and the children were dressed up as saints.

"Who remembers what we learned about the saints?" Miss Diaz asked.

Miss Diaz saw Jamal raise his hand and she asked him to tell the class. Jamal said, "The saints were God's special helpers."

"That's right, Jamal," said Miss Diaz. "The saints were God's special helpers. They told people how much God loves them. Now they live with God in Heaven."

"I'm dressed up like Saint Francis," said Jamal. "He loved animals."

Kim said, "I'm Saint Thérèse. My mom says that people also call her the 'Little Flower.' "

"Carlos, who are you dressed up as?" Miss Diaz asked Carlos. "I'm Saint Juan Diego. He was born in Mexico, just like me," Carlos proudly told everyone.

"Wow!" said Abby. "I like all the costumes. Mine is Saint Elizabeth. My mom said she was a teacher who taught children about Jesus."

"Boys and girls, you all look so wonderful. It's time to go to church for our special celebration. Is everyone ready?" Miss Diaz gave the signal, and Jamal, Kim, Abby, Carlos and all their classmates walked to the church. They would walk down the aisle and sit together in the very front rows.

All their parents and friends would be there. Together they would thank God for all the wonderful saints who showed us ways to live as friends of Jesus.

Welcome

- Provide a set of puzzle pieces made from copies of the activity master found on page 162 in the guide, one set for each of the children.
- Greet the children by name and direct them to the Welcome Center. Show the children a completed puzzle that you have made. Ask the children to take a set of puzzle pieces and put the puzzle together.
- Walk among the children as they are putting their puzzles together. Help the children who need your assistance.
- Talk with the children about the picture on their completed puzzle. Explain that the picture shows a child being kind to another child.
- Summarize that Jesus told us that his friends are to be kind to other people.

Gather

Play the gathering song to signal that it is time for the children to clean up and move to the Story Time Area.

Teach

Introduce the story.

- Call the children's attention to the teaching poster or show them the cover of the children's leaflet. Point to the title "All Saints Day." Point specifically to the word *Saints* and say it aloud. Ask the children to echo the word *Saints* after you.
- Explain to the children that saints are people who live in Heaven with Jesus. They are God's special helpers who were kind to people.
- Invite them to listen *(point to illustration)* to today's story to discover why Kim, Carlos, Abby and Jamal are dressed up the way they are.

Tell the story.

Tell the children the name of today's story "Dressing Up as Saints." Refer to the teaching poster or the cover of the children's leaflet as you read the story to the children.

Recall the story.

- Help the children recall the key details of the story.
- Ask these questions:
  - Who were the children in Miss Diaz's class dressed as? *(saints)*
  - Who are the saints? *(The saints are God's special helpers. They live with God in Heaven.)*
  - Why did Jamal, Kim, Abby and Carlos dress up as saints? *(They dressed up for a special celebration in church.)*
- Conclude by pointing to the teaching poster or children's leaflet. Remind the children, "The name of the celebration Jamal, Kim, Abby and Carlos were dressed up for is called "All Saints Day."

- Summarize by reminding the children that saints live with God in Heaven. They show us how to live as friends of Jesus.

 ## Apply

Work on the children's leaflet activity.

- Have several children help you hand out the children's leaflet for this chapter. Call attention to the cover to help them remember why Jamal, Kim, Abby and Carlos were dressed up.
- Ask the children to open their leaflet. Call their attention to the title "Saint Francis of Assisi" and have them look at the illustration of Saint Francis on the center pages. Remind the children that Jamal was dressed up as Saint Francis.
- Share with the children that Saint Francis knew how much God loved him and everyone. He knew that God was kind to everyone. Saint Francis was kind to people and kind to animals. Whenever Saint Francis heard birds sing or saw beautiful flowers or any of the wonderful things in the world, he knew how much God loved him. All these things showed Saint Francis how kind God is to us.
- Call the children's attention to the picture and ask them to finish coloring the picture as a reminder that God loves them very much. Conclude by asking the children to thank God for St. Francis and all the saints.

Connect with the child's life.

- Tell the children to take their puzzles home. Show your completed puzzle and say, "Jesus asks all his friends, and that includes you and me, to be kind. We are to be kind to our family and friends, to our teachers and classmates. We are to be kind to our pets and other animals. We are to be kind to all God's creatures." Ask:
    —What can you do to be kind at home?
    —What can you do to be kind to your friends?
    —What can you do to be kind to your pets and other animals?
- Remind the children to take home their leaflet and to share the story on the For My Family Page and the activity with their families.

Saint Francis of Assisi

Finish coloring the pictures.
Thank God for Saint Francis and all the saints.

 ## Pray

- Gather the children at the prayer table.
- Quiet the children by having them repeat after you, "My head I bow. / My hands I fold. / Now I talk to God." *(Pause.)*
- Introduce the prayer. Remind the children that the saints are God's special helpers who now live with him in Heaven. They help us live as friends of Jesus. Explain to the children that in today's prayer we will ask the saints to help us live as friends of Jesus. They will pray "Thank you, God, for giving us the saints" after you each time you pray those words.
- Lead the children in prayer. Begin with the Sign of the Cross.

Teacher:	God our Father, you give us the saints. We now ask the saints to help us live as friends of Jesus.
Teacher:	Saint Francis, help us live as friends of Jesus. Thank you, God, for giving us the saints.
All:	Thank you . . .
Teacher:	Saint Thérèse, help us live as friends of Jesus. Thank you, God, for giving us the saints.
All:	Thank you . . .
Teacher:	Saint Juan Diego, help us live as friends of Jesus. Thank you, God, for giving us the saints.
All:	Thank you . . .
Teacher:	Saint Elizabeth, help us live as friends of Jesus. Thank you, God, for giving us the saints.
All:	Thank you . . .
Teacher:	Together let us pray, "Amen."
All:	Amen.

Additional Activity

Learn and sing a song about the saints.

Use this activity to help the children sing a song of thanks for the saints.

- Explain to the children that you will teach them a song about the saints. Tell them that you will sing the song one line at a time. Then they will sing that line with you.
- Practice singing the song with the children. Sing the lyrics to the tune of "When the Saints Go Marching In."
    We thank you, God, for all the saints.
    We thank you, God, for all the saints.
    For they taught us how you love us.
    Thank you, God, for all the saints.
- Option: Practice and sing "When the Saints Go Marching In" with the children.
- Lead the children in singing the song. Then invite them to stand and sing the song as they follow you as you march around the room. Optional: You might sing this song to conclude the prayer.

Thanksgiving Day

Background
for the Catechist

Give Thanks, Always Give Thanks

"Give thanks to the LORD on the harp; / on the ten-stringed lyre offer praise" (Psalm 33:2). Thanking and praising God flows naturally from the hearts of the people of God. The experience of the lavishness of God's love revealed and made present in Christ stirred the heart of Saint Paul to proclaim, "Thanks be to God for his indescribable gift!" (2 Corinthians 9:15) and to enjoin all Christians, "In all circumstances give thanks" (1 Thessalonians 5:18).

On Thanksgiving Day in the United States of America, the Church raises her voice in prayer, "Father, / we do well to join all creation, / in [H]eaven and on earth, / in praising you, our mighty God / through Jesus Christ our Lord" (*Roman Missal,* Preface, Thanksgiving Day).

We remember that God wishes all people to be blessed and all people to be free. We join to thank God for all his blessings and the gift of freedom. We thank him for the gift of freedom in the Holy Spirit who empowers us to proclaim the blessed vision of peace he desires for the world.

For Reflection

In what ways do I live a life of thanks all year long for my blessings, especially the blessing of freedom? What can I do to help the children understand that all good things come from God and to help them give thanks to him?

About the Children

Three- and four-year-olds love to be with other children and are learning to share toys and play cooperatively. You might also notice that the children will withhold or take their friendship back when other children do something that they do not like. For example, you might hear them protest, "I won't be your friend if you . . ." or "You can't come to my party if you don't . . ." Helping the children deal with these feelings and the way they express them is key to helping the children grow socially.

A Few Suggestions . . .

It is important to plan and develop a learning environment that supports the social development of the children. Take advantage of the many small group projects and opportunities for cooperative learning in the *Stories of God's Love* lesson plans. Consistently draw the children's attention away from being self-focused and toward the recognition of the needs of others. Work with the children so that they can see concrete ways that their behavior impacts others, both positively and negatively. Establish clear expectations for respectful interactions and remind the children of these expectations when they forget them.

More Background

For further reading and reflection see *Catechism of the Catholic Church* §§ 2402, 2443–2449, 2637–2643, 2828–2837; *Compendium— Catechism of the Catholic Church* §§ 503, 520, 555– 556, 592–593; *United States Catholic Catechism for Adults* pages 421–425, 468, 487.

Lesson Planner

Faith Focus

We thank God for all his blessings.

Story

"The Thank-You Game"

Enriching the Lesson

- RCL Benziger *Stories of God's Love* Music CD and companion Songbook, Song 1
- Visit our preschool Web site www.RCLBenzigerPreschool.com this week.

Chapter Objectives

After this week's lesson the children should be able to:

- recall the story "The Thank-You Game."
- discover that on Thanksgiving Day we give thanks to God for all his blessings.
- thank God for all his blessings.

Materials Needed

In addition to the general supplies named on page 9 of this guide, you will need the following materials for teaching this lesson:

- poster board with simple outline drawing of cornucopia
- fruit and vegetable shapes cut out from the activity master on page 163 of this guide, one set for each of the children
- fruits, fall vegetables, pictures of families, Bible and so on to place on prayer table

Prayer

Almighty God,
to you belongs all that is good.
We hold the riches of the universe
only in trust.
Make us honest stewards of your creation,
compassionate and just in sharing its bounty
with the whole human family.
Amen.

FROM *A BOOK OF PRAYERS*

The Thank-You Game

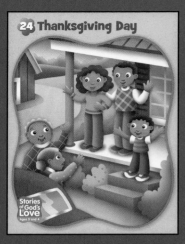

"Thanksgiving Day! I love it!" shouted Jamal to his mom and dad. "When do we get to eat? I want the drumstick from the turkey and lots of mashed potatoes. Can we eat now?"

"Hold on, Son. We need to wait for Grandpa, Aunt Cala and Uncle Adel and Cousin Isa. When everyone is here, we can eat," said Dad.

"I have an idea," said Mom. "While we are waiting, let's take turns talking about all of the things we are thankful for. I'll start. I am thankful for my family. I love you both so much."

"My turn, my turn," said Jamal. "I am thankful for you, Mom and Dad, and for my favorite cousin Isa."

"I'm thankful for both of you and for God's love," added Dad.

"This is fun. I love Thanksgiving Day!" said Jamal. "I'm thinking of lots of things. I think I'll pick Grandpa! Yes, I am thankful for Grandpa."

Beep! Beep! They heard a car coming up the road that leads to the barn. "They're here! They're here!" shouted Jamal. "I'm thankful they're here. Now we can eat!"

Mom and Dad and Jamal all headed out to welcome everyone. Yes, Thanksgiving Day would be a wonderful day for Jamal and his family.

 Welcome

- Provide a simple outline of a cornucopia on a large piece of poster board, fruit and vegetable shapes cut out from the activity master found on page 163 in this guide, one set for each of the children, and glue or paste.
- Greet the children by name and direct them to the Welcome Center. Show the poster board on which you have pasted the shape of a fruit and of a vegetable on the cornucopia. Tell the children this is a cornucopia. The things we fill it with remind us of all the good things God gives us. Say the word *cornucopia* aloud and have the children echo it after you.
- Hand out a set of fruit and vegetable shapes to each of the children. Have them color the shapes and paste or glue them to the cornucopia.
- Walk among the children as they are coloring and explain the meaning of Thanksgiving Day. Tell them that on Thanksgiving Day we remember all of God's blessings to us. Tell them that we use the word *blessings* to name all the good things God gives us. Help the children paste their fruit and vegetable shapes in the cornucopia when they finish coloring them.
- Bring the cornucopia poster to the Story Time Area and display it there.

 Gather

- Play the gathering song to signal that it is time for the children to clean up and move to the Story Time Area.
- Invite the children to tell about one of the items they attached to the cornucopia poster. Remind the children that all good things come from God. They are blessings from God.

 Teach

Introduce the story.

- Call the children's attention to the teaching poster or to the cover of the children's leaflet. Ask the children to name the *Stories of God's Love* character in the illustration. *(Jamal)*
- Point to and read aloud the title "Thanksgiving Day" and invite the children to listen to the story about Jamal to discover the game he and his family played on Thanksgiving Day.

Tell the story.

Begin reading the story to the children. Note: Do not read the name of the story since it names the game Jamal and his family play. Refer to the teaching poster or the cover of the children's leaflet as you read the story to the children.

Recall the story.

- Help the children recall the story by asking and congratulating them for their responses to these questions.

—What was the special day in the story that Jamal and his family were celebrating? *(Thanksgiving Day)*

—What did Jamal's family decide to do while they were waiting for their company? *(Play the "thank-you" game)*

—What was Jamal thankful for? *(Mom and Dad, Grandpa and cousin)*

- Summarize by telling the children, "We thank God in a special way on Thanksgiving Day for all our blessings. But we need to remember to thank God every day for our blessings."

 ## Apply

Work on the children's leaflet activity.

- Have several children help you hand out the children's leaflet for chapter 24. Give the children time to examine the cover to help them recall the story.
- Ask them to open their leaflet. Call their attention to the title "We Give Thanks" and read it aloud to the children. Tell the children the pictures they see are pictures of just some things God gives us that we all thank God for.
- Invite them to talk about the pictures and share some of the other things they are thankful for. Encourage the children to share ideas by asking them about their favorite foods, what they most enjoy doing with their family and the friends they like to play with.
- Explain the directions for the activity and ask the children to begin coloring their placemat.
- Walk among the children as they are coloring. Remind the children that all these good things are blessings from God. They are all things we are to thank God for each and every day.

Connect with the child's life.

- Ask the children, "What can you thank God for when you pray your bedtime prayers tonight?"
- Remind the children to take home their leaflet and to share the story "The Thank-You Game" on the For My Family Page and the activity with their families. Encourage them to play the thank-you game that Jamal and his family played.

We Give Thanks

Thank You, God.

Color the pictures.
Pray "Thank you, God."

 ## Pray

- Place on the prayer table a variety of items that will remind the children to say thank you to God, for example, fruits, fall vegetables, pictures of families, a Bible and so on.
- Gather the children at the prayer table. Explain to the children that they will sing their prayer today. Tell them you will first teach them the prayer and practice singing it with them.
- Practice singing this prayer with the children to the tune of "Are You Sleeping?"

    It's Thanksgiving . . . We give thanks . . .
    For the many good gifts . . . Thank you, God.

- Call the children to a moment of silence. *(Pause.)* Lead them in prayer. Begin with the Sign of the Cross.

Additional Activities

Make a prayer tube.
Use this activity to encourage the children to see all of the wonderful gifts, or blessings, that God has given us.

- Provide blunt scissors, glue, wrapping-paper tubes or paper-towel tubes taped together, one for each of the children, and magazines or other sources of pictures that depict things that three- and four-year-olds might be thankful for. Make a prayer, using the directions below.
- Show the children a completed prayer tube you have made. Ask the children to work together to make a prayer tube like yours. Invite them to look through the magazines to find a picture that shows something that they wish to thank God for. Then have them cut out their pictures and glue them to the tube. Be sure to help those children who need assistance cutting and gluing.
- Let the children take turns holding the tube as they say a thank-you prayer to God.

Say a thank-you prayer.
Use this activity to help the children say thank you to God for all of the good gifts they have.

- Provide a bag that has a drawstring tie and contains small animal and people figures, plastic fruits and vegetables and so on.
- Show the children the bag filled with the figures and explain the activity to them. Tell them that you will call them by name, one at a time. They are to come up and reach into the bag and take out one of the items. They are to show the item to the class and everyone will pray aloud, "Thank you, God, for *(name of item)*."
- Demonstrate the activity and then invite the children to take turns reaching into the bag and taking out one of the items.

CHAPTER 25

Getting Ready for Christmas

Background
for the Catechist

The Coming of the Lord

Advent begins the celebration of the liturgical year of the Church. The Advent season is a time of preparation that is filled with anticipation and hope.

Throughout the four Sundays of Advent, we listen to the Old Testament prophets. Isaiah, Jeremiah, Baruch, Zephaniah and Micah share the longing of God's people for the coming of the Messiah and Savior promised by God.

The Sunday Gospel readings move us ever closer to the fulfillment of that promise. We are told, "Be watchful! Be alert!" (Mark 13:33). John the Baptist announces his coming, "[T]he one who is coming after me is mightier than I" (Matthew 3:11). The angel Gabriel, sent by God, announces to Mary, "Behold, you will conceive in your womb and bear a son, and you shall name him Jesus. He will be great and will be called Son of the Most High" (Luke 1:31–32).

Advent favors quiet anticipation. An extra effort is needed to offset the pre-Christmas hustle and bustle. Advent invites us to prepare patiently, quietly and with an awareness of the coming of Jesus Christ here and now, with the assurance that God is always with us for his name is E-man-u-el, "God is with us" (Matthew 1:23).

For Reflection

How does celebrating the Advent season help me live in the mystery of God's presence? What can I do to help the children develop a sense of quiet and patient waiting for the celebration of Christmas?

About the Children

Advent is a time of great anticipation. While children often want things "now," they are great anticipators. They look forward to events, such as birthday celebrations, trips to a park, time with their friends, visits from grandparents and cousins and other family members, with an anticipation that contributes to their celebration of events. Build on their looking forward to Christmas. Building on such expressions as "I can't wait for Christmas," you can help your child celebrate the seasons of both Advent and Christmas in a meaningful and joyful way.

A Few Suggestions . . .

One way to help the children manage their feelings of anticipation and excitement is to have them participate in "mini-celebrations." Help the children celebrate and come to enjoy the Advent season as a series of fun and meaningful activities versus a focus on a four-week period of waiting for Christmas Day. For example, use the Advent calendar in this week's leaflet as a way of communicating with the children about the special activities that will be happening during the Advent season. Include the children in parish celebrations, such as the lighting of the Advent candle or the celebration of Las Posadas and other special Advent activities.

More Background

For further reading and reflection see *Catechism of the Catholic Church* §§ 522–524, 748, 2466; *Compendium—Catechism of the Catholic Church* § 102; *United States Catholic Catechism for Adults* pages 173, 503.

Lesson Planner

Faith Focus

During Advent the friends of Jesus prepare for and look forward to the celebration of his birth.

Bible Story

"The Angel Tells Mary Wonderful News" (Based on Luke 1:26–31, 36, 45–46)

Materials Needed

In addition to the general supplies named on page 9 of this guide, you will need the following materials for teaching this lesson:

- construction paper cut into 2-inch wide strips, several strips for each of the children
- closed Bible with bookmark placed at Luke 1:26-46
- Advent wreath

Enriching the Lesson

- RCL Benziger *Stories of God's Love* Music CD and companion Songbook, Song 1
- Visit our preschool Web site www.RCLBenzigerPreschool.com this week.

Chapter Objectives

After this week's lesson the children should be able to:

- recall the Bible story, "The Angel Tells Mary Wonderful News."
- discover that the time we prepare for Christmas is called Advent.
- ask God to help them get ready to celebrate the birth of Jesus at Christmas.

Prayer

Father in Heaven,
increase our longing for Christ your Son.
Send the Holy Spirit
to strengthen us to grow in love
and find us rejoicing in his presence
when he comes.
Amen.

BASED ON *ROMAN MISSAL*, ALTERNATIVE OPENING PRAYER, FIRST SUNDAY OF ADVENT

25 Getting Ready for Christmas

Stories of God's Love
Ages 3 and 4

The Angel Tells Mary Wonderful News

One day Mary was in her home. Mary lived in a town named Nazareth. While she was there, God sent the angel Gabriel to her. The angel said to Mary, "Greetings, Mary, God loves you very much. You are very special to God."

At first Mary was very surprised to hear the angel speaking to her. Then the angel told Mary this wonderful message from God. The angel said, "You are blessed, Mary. Do not be afraid. God the Father has chosen you to be the Mother of his Son. The Holy Spirit will come to you. You will have a baby. You will give him the name Jesus. Your child will be God's own Son."

Mary knew that God loved her. She told the angel, "Tell God that I will do what he wants me to do." Mary said yes to God.

Then the angel told her that her cousin Elizabeth was also going to have a baby. After the angel left her, Mary went to visit her cousin Elizabeth. When Elizabeth saw Mary coming, she greeted Mary, saying, "Mary, God has blessed you very much."

Mary said, "God is so good and great. I am so happy that he has blessed me so much."

BASED ON LUKE 1:26–32, 36, 45–46

 Welcome

- Provide twenty-four pieces of construction paper (one for each of the days of the Advent season) cut into 2-inch wide strips and tape or a stapler.
- Greet the children by name and direct them to the Welcome Center. Show the children several construction paper strips that you made in preparation of this lesson on Advent.
- Explain that you made the decorations to help decorate the classroom to get ready for the celebration of Christmas. Tell them that the time we have to get ready to celebrate Christmas is called Advent. Say the word *Advent* aloud again and have the children echo it after you.
- Explain the activity to the children. Tell them, "One way we can get ready for celebrating Christmas is to put up decorations that remind us that Christmas is coming." Show them the construction paper strips you decorated and explain to them that they are going to decorate strips too and that you will help them put all the strips together to make a paper chain to decorate the room.
- Hand out the paper strips and invite the children to use crayons or markers to decorate the strips. Let the children take turns coming up and assisting you in taping or stapling the strips into a chain.

 Gather

- Play the gathering song to signal that it is time for the children to clean up and move to the Story Time Area.
- Lead the children in singing an age-appropriate hymn that your parish traditionally sings during Advent.

 Teach

Introduce the Bible story.

Call the children's attention to the teaching poster or the cover of the children's leaflet. Tell the children that today you will tell them a Bible story about Mary hearing very good news. Invite the children to listen to the Bible story to discover the good news Mary heard.

Tell the Bible story.

Invite a child to come up and open the Bible to the place marked by the bookmark, Luke 1:26-46. Take the opened Bible, place the children's leaflet inside. Tell the children the name of the Bible story "The Angel Tells Mary Wonderful News." Refer to the teaching poster or the cover of the children's leaflet as you read the Bible story on the For My Family Page to the children.

Recall the Bible story.

- Help the children recall the key details of the Bible story. Explain to them that you will need their help to remember the story. Read each of the following statements and when you come to the missing word ask, "Who can tell me the missing word?"

- Read each of the incomplete statements aloud, providing clues as necessary to help the children recall the story:
  —Mary heard some good news from an ____. *(angel)*
  —The angel told Mary she would have a ____. *(baby boy)*
  —The angel told Mary, "You will give your baby the name ____." *(Jesus)*
  —The angel then told Mary, "Your Son is also the Son of ____. *(God)*
- Remind the children that Mary had to get ready for the birth of Jesus. Tell them that we get ready to celebrate the birth of Jesus in the Church at Christmas. We call this time that we get ready for Christmas Advent.
- Say the word *Advent* aloud and have the children echo it after you.

 ## Apply

Work on the children's leaflet activity.

- Have several children help you hand out the children's leaflet for this chapter. Call their attention to the cover to help them recall the Bible story.
- Ask the children to open their leaflet. Call their attention to the title and read it aloud to them. Ask them to look at the illustration on the center pages and tell them that what they see is called an Advent calendar. Have them echo the words after you.
- Tell the children that we use an Advent calendar to help us get ready to celebrate Christmas.
- Explain the directions to the children and have them begin coloring their calendars.
- Walk among the children as they are working. Point to the calendars and share with them that Advent lasts for four weeks.
- Tell them that they will finish their calendar with their family at home.

Connect with the child's life.

- Encourage the children to share the new word *(Advent)* that they learned today with their parents. Remind them that this is a time of preparation and waiting before Christmas.
- Remind the children to take home their leaflet and to share the Bible story and their Advent calendar with their family.

 ## Pray

- Display an Advent wreath on the prayer table.
- Call the children's attention to the Advent wreath and remind them of its purpose. Explain to the children that in their prayer today they will ask God to help them get ready for Christmas. Tell them that you will say the words of the prayer and they will echo the words after you.
- Gather the children near the prayer table. Call for a moment of silence. *(Pause.)* Lead the children in prayer. Begin with the Sign of the Cross.
  Dear God, *(Children echo the words.)*
  we are getting ready for Christmas.
    (Children echo the words.)
  Christmas is coming soon. *(Children echo the words.)*
  Help us to be kind and to pray each day. Amen.
  (Children echo the words.)
- Conclude the prayer by singing the Advent hymn that you sang with the children during the gathering time.

Additional Activity

Prepare for Christmas.
Use this activity to reinforce the concept that we decorate for Christmas.

- In advance make cinnamon dough by combining 1½ C. ground cinnamon, 1 C. applesauce and ½ C. white glue. Mix in bowl and knead until dough forms into a ball. Let mixture sit for 30 minutes. Also provide a rolling pin, blunt knife, straws, wax paper, religious-theme cookie cutters, yarn and a small Christmas tree.
- Tell the children they will work together to make decorations to get ready during Advent to celebrate Christmas. Dust your hands, the rolling pin and cookie cutters with cinnamon to prevent sticking. Using the rolling pin, flatten the dough to ½-inch thickness.
- Help the children press the cookie cutters into the dough and use the blunt knife to cut out ornaments. Then use a straw to make a hole in the top of each shape.
- Lay the shapes on wax paper to dry, turning them daily for five days. Assist the children in putting yarn through the holes and hanging the ornaments on the tree.

CHAPTER 26

We Celebrate Christmas

Background
for the Catechist

The Search of the Magi

A life of communion and friendship with God is the purpose and destiny of every human life. The great Saint Augustine put it this way, "Our hearts are restless, O God, until they rest in you."

The search of the Magi, the wise men from the East, is the search of every person. Leaving the comfort and security of their homeland, the Magi follow a light, a star, in search of a newborn king. They discover an infant not in royal garb in a palace in the presence of a royal family but a child in swaddling clothes lying in a manger in the presence of an artisan from Nazareth and his wife, Mary.

Christmas is the assurance that God desires and makes possible the success of our search for him. The Incarnation and the birth of the Son of God brought the light that guides our search for God into the world. Jesus, true God and true man, the Light of the world, guides and makes possible the success of our search for God. In Christ, with him, and through him, life with God is made possible.

For Reflection

In what ways do I actively search for Jesus in my daily life? What do I say and do while I am with the children that show that living as a friend of Jesus is at the center of my life?

About the Children

Young children learn new concepts by connecting them to concepts that are part of their experience and existing knowledge. When presented with new ideas and situations, children will strive to make connections with what they already know and have experienced. Helping children make connections to their prior knowledge is critical to their learning new ideas and skills.

A Few Suggestions . . .

Teachers and parents can facilitate new learning by providing the opportunities for children to take part in activities that help them discover and make connections between new concepts and existing knowledge. In this week's lesson, children will learn about the concept "honor," which is a very abstract term for preschoolers. You might connect the idea of honor with the children's knowledge and experience of showing their parents and other adults respect. For example, when a child addresses you as Mr. or Mrs., say to them, "Thank you for showing respect by addressing me as Mrs. (or Mr.). You honor me when you do." This will help the children discover the meaning of honor by connecting it with their experience of showing respect.

More Background

For further reading and reflection see *Catechism of the Catholic Church* §§ 1–3, 27–30, 519–521, 528, 1171; *Compendium—Catechism of the Catholic Church* §§ 2, 101, 103; *United States Catholic Catechism for Adults* pages 2–3, 81–83, 173.

Lesson Planner

Faith Focus

The Magi honor Jesus, the Son of God and Son of Mary.

Bible Story

"The Magi Visit the Baby Jesus" (Based on Matthew 2:1–2, 9–11)

Materials Needed

In addition to the general supplies named on page 9 of this guide, you will need the following materials for teaching this lesson:

- paper cut into two triangles, one set of triangles for each of the children
- glitter and stickers
- closed Bible with bookmark placed at Matthew 1:1–11

Enriching the Lesson

- RCL Benziger *Stories of God's Love* Music CD and companion Songbook, Song 1
- Visit our preschool Web site www.RCLBenzigerPreschool.com this week.

Chapter Objectives

After this week's lesson the children should be able to:

- recall the Bible story "The Magi Visit the Baby Jesus."
- discover that they can honor Jesus when they are kind to others.
- honor Jesus by praying.

Prayer

Loving God,
bless us with your presence
as we celebrate this season
of wonder and awe.
Send the Holy Spirit
to keep alive in our minds and hearts
that you are always with us.
Amen.

26 We Celebrate Christmas

Stories of God's Love
Ages 3 and 4

The Magi Visit the Baby Jesus

When the time came for Jesus to be born, he was born in the city of Bethlehem. Since there was no place for Mary and Joseph to stay in Bethlehem, Jesus was born in a place where people kept animals.

Soon after Jesus was born, wise men traveled very far to find the baby Jesus to honor him. The wise men are also called Magi.

"Where is the special child who was born?" the Magi asked when they came near Jerusalem. "We have seen his star and we have come to honor him as a king."

"Go to the city of Bethlehem," they were told. "You will find the child you are looking for there."

When they came near to Bethlehem, the Magi saw the star they were following. It had stopped in the sky over the place where Jesus was born.

Going into the place where Jesus was, the Magi saw Jesus with his Mother, Mary, and they knelt down before them.

The Magi took out the three very special gifts of gold and frankincense and myrrh that they brought with them and gave them to Jesus to honor him.

BASED ON MATTHEW 2:1–2, 9–11

 Welcome

- Provide paper triangle shapes, two for each of the children, glue, markers and crayons, glitter and other decorative materials.
- Greet the children by name and direct them to the Welcome Center.
- Show the children a decorated star shape that you have made in preparation for teaching the lesson. Tell the children it is a special Christmas star and that you will work with them to help them make their own Christmas stars.
- Hand out two paper triangle shapes to each of the children. Show them how to invert the two triangles by having one triangle point upward and the other triangle point downward. Then show them how to place one triangle shape on top of the other to make a star. Assist them in gluing the two shapes together to make a star. Invite the children to decorate their star using the markers, crayons and other materials.

 Gather

- Play the gathering song to signal that it is time for the children to clean up and move to the Story Time Area.
- Have the children bring the Christmas stars they made to the Story Time Area. Lead the children in singing a hymn that your parish traditionally sings during the Christmas season, for example, "We Three Kings" or "What Star Is This," or have them sing this song to the tune of "Twinkle, Twinkle Little Star."

  Twinkle, twinkle little star, / The Magi saw you from afar. / Up above our Savior's bed, / Where Baby Jesus laid his head. / Twinkle, twinkle little star, / The Magi saw you from afar.

- Practice singing the song with the children. Then lead them in singing it. Invite them to wave their stars as they sing.

 Teach

Introduce the Bible story.

Show the children the teaching poster or the cover of the children's leaflet for this chapter. Tell the children that today you will read a Bible story to them. Read the title of the Bible story "The Magi Visit the Baby Jesus" to them. Say the word *Magi* out loud again and have the children echo the word *Magi* after you. Show them the Christmas star you made and ask them to listen to discover what the Bible story tells them about the Christmas star.

Tell the Bible story.

- Invite a child to come up and open the Bible to the place marked by the bookmark, Matthew 2:1–11. Take the opened Bible, place the children's leaflet inside. Refer to the teaching poster or the cover of the children's leaflet as you read the Bible story to the children.

- Pause after you read the word *honor* in the Bible story and explain to the children that to honor someone means to do or say something that shows someone respect. Have the children echo the word *honor* before you continue reading the story.

Recall the Bible story.

- Help the children recall key elements of the Bible story. Tell them that you will ask them three questions about the Bible story. You will stop after each question and, if they know the answer to the question, they are to hold up and wave their Christmas star. You then will ask everyone who knows the answer to say the answer out loud.
- Ask the children to respond to these questions:
  —What did the Magi follow to the place where Jesus stayed? *(a star)*
  —Why did the Magi come to visit Jesus? *(to honor him)*
- Name the special gifts the Magi brought. *(gold, frankincense and myrrh)* Say them aloud and have the children echo the words after you. Note: Frankincense and myrrh are resins from trees. When burned they produce strong, sweet aromas.

 Apply

Work on the children's leaflet activity.

- Have several children help you hand out the children's leaflet for this chapter. Have everyone briefly look at the cover and then open their leaflet. Call their attention to the activity. Explain it to them.
- Ask the children to use their finger to lead the Magi along the road to Jesus and Mary. Then invite them to use a marker or a crayon to color the path from the Magi to Jesus and Mary and then to color the presents.
- Conclude by telling the children that the Magi showed their love and honor for Jesus by kneeling before him and giving him the special gifts.

Help the Magi Find Jesus

Color and follow the path from the Magi to the Baby Jesus.
Tell Jesus you love him.

Connect with the child's life.

- Tell the children they honor Jesus by giving him the gift of their love. Remind them of the song "Little Drummer Boy" and how he showed his love for Jesus. Ask them. "What is one thing you can do to show your love for Jesus?"
- Remind the children to take their leaflet home and to share the story and the activity with their family.
- Give the children the Christmas stars they made to take home. Encourage them to ask their parents to put the star in a special place in their home to honor Jesus.

 Pray

- Display a Christmas creche on the prayer table.
- Gather the children at the prayer table. Explain to the children that in the prayer they will pray the words after you. Say, "We honor you" aloud and have them say the words aloud after you.
- Call the children to a moment of silence. *(Pause.)* Invite a child to come to the prayer table and open the Bible to the place marked by the bookmark, Matthew 2:11. Reverently take the Bible and lead the children in prayer. Begin with the Sign of the Cross.

Teacher:	Let us listen and remember what the Magi did to honor Baby Jesus. *Read aloud,* "The Magi knelt down and gave Jesus gifts to honor Jesus" *(Based on Matthew 2:11).*
Teacher:	Jesus, you are God's own Son. We honor you.
Children:	*Echo the words* "We honor you."
Teacher:	Jesus, you are Mary's only Son. We honor you.
Children:	*Echo the words* "We honor you."
Teacher:	We give you the gift of our love. We honor you. Amen.
Children:	*Echo the words* "We honor you. Amen."

Additional Activity

Follow the Star Game.

Use this activity to help the children recall the story of the visit of the Magi.

- Provide several footprints and a large star made from the patterns on the activity master found on pages 164 and 165 of this guide. Create a simple path in the learning area by taping the footprints to the floor. Have the path lead to the teaching poster for this week or the front cover of the children's leaflet over which you have displayed the star.
- Invite the children to take turns following the footprints to the star, saying, "We come to honor Jesus."

CHAPTER 27 Valentine's Day

Background
for the Catechist

No Greater Love

Saint Valentine was a third-century bishop who tradition teaches sacrificed his life to protect Christians who wished to marry. Most of us today are not called upon to literally lay down our life for others or for faith in Jesus Christ as Bishop Valentine did.

We are called, however, to love others as Jesus loves us. By the way we love one another others will know we are his disciples. (See John 13:34.) What does "to love as Jesus loves us" require of us? Jesus himself described that love when he taught, "No one has greater love than this, to lay down one's life for one's friends" (John 15:13).

The hallmark of the life of a disciple of Christ is laying down our life for others as Jesus did. The life of a disciple of Christ includes putting our life on the line for God and for others each and every day. In small and great ways we lay down our life for our family, friends, neighbors and strangers as each situation invites us. Our friendship with Christ is so deep that we strive to respond to every situation by loving one another as Jesus would. Saint Valentine is one of the many disciples of Christ whose life gives witness to the sacrificial love required of all Christians.

For Reflection

What are some of the daily invitations that invite me to "lay down" my life for family, friends, neighbors and strangers? In what ways do I see the children loving one another as Jesus taught? What can I do to affirm their efforts?

More Background

For further reading and reflection see *Catechism of the Catholic Church* §§ 459, 478, 828, 1337, 1822–1829; *Compendium— Catechism of the Catholic Church* §§ 85, 93, 388; *United States Catholic Catechism for Adults* pages 91–92, 286.

About the Children

What does it mean to love the children we serve? True love is a balance of unconditional acceptance and setting limits. It involves responding to a child by both giving and denying. Children often balk at the limits that parents and teachers set for them. On the other hand, limits also provide security, safety and predictability. All these factors establish a consistency that enables children to thrive and grow. Sometimes adults think that they are making a child happy when they forego consistency and a predictable routine in order to quiet a crying child. The opposite, however, is true. Inconsistency in the way adults respond to a child's needs and demands creates an environment that the child will experience as unsafe and insecure.

A Few Suggestions . . .

Setting up predictable classroom routines can help young children feel safe and secure. In addition to predictable routines, young children also need to be able to predict how the adults in their life will react to situations. Be consistent in your responses to the children. Avoid sending mixed signals. Expect consistent adherence to classroom rules. Your consistent and predictable responses to the children will build a loving environment, a safe and secure environment, in which the children best learn.

Lesson Planner

Faith Focus

We do what Jesus told us to do when we are kind to people and help them.

Story

"A Valentine's Day Hug"

Enriching the Lesson

- RCL Benziger *Stories of God's Love* Music CD and companion Songbook, Song 1
- Visit our preschool Web site www.RCLBenzigerPreschool.com this week.

Chapter Objectives

After this week's lesson the children should be able to:

- recall the story "A Valentine's Day Hug."
- discover ways to show their love for someone else by helping them and being kind to them.
- celebrate their love for family and friends.

Materials Needed

In addition to the general supplies named on page 9 of this guide, you will need the following materials for teaching this lesson:

- heart shapes cut from copies of activity master on pages 166 and 167 of this guide, several for each of the children
- construction paper and strips of paper with words "Love one another" on them, enough materials for each of the children

Prayer

Blessed are you, God of all love.
Out of love
you have sent your Son, Jesus.
Out of love you have called me
to be a disciple of your Son.
Send the Holy Spirit
to strengthen me to return your love
with all my heart, mind and soul.
Amen.

A Valentine's Day Hug

Carlos was cutting out a big red heart to put on his bedroom door. Dad drew it, and Carlos was carefully cutting around the edges. Valentine's Day was tomorrow. Dad made cookies and put red icing on them while Mom was at work.

"Remember," Dad said, "Valentine's Day is a special day. It reminds us to show our love to our family and friends. It is nice to think of kind things we will do for them."

"I'm going to give Mom a flower tomorrow when she gets home from work," Carlos said, "and tell her how much I love her."

"That's wonderful. I'm going to tell Mom how much I love her too," Dad added. "Who else do you love?"

"I love Grandpa. I love him a lot," Carlos said. "I think when we go to the park next time I'll let him go down the slide first."

"Oh, Grandpa will love that! And don't forget to say 'I love you' to him too," Dad said.

Carlos nodded and said, "In school, Miss Diaz told us who loves us the most. Do you know who that is, Dad?"

"I think God loves us the most. And you know what else? I think we show God how much we love him when we show our love to our friends and family by being kind to them and helping them," Dad said.

"Yep, that's just what Miss Diaz said. You know what, Dad? I love you. I don't want to wait until tomorrow. I want to give you a big hug right now!" Carlos wrapped his arms around his dad.

"I like that," said Dad. "I love you too."

Welcome

- Provide crayons and glue, a variety of heart shapes cut from copies of the activity master found on page 166 of this guide, several different sizes for each of the children. Also provide a sheet of construction paper and the sentence strip "Love one another" printed on the activity master found on page 167.
- Greet the children by name and direct them to the Welcome Center. Show them the heart shapes and remind them that the heart shapes remind us that Jesus told us to love one another.
- Hand out the construction paper and have the children choose several heart shapes and arrange them on the construction paper.
- Show the children a sentence strip and read the words printed on it to the children. Assist them in gluing the heart shapes and the sentence strip to their papers.
- Collect the completed papers to give to the children to take home.

Gather

- Play the gathering song to signal that it is time for the children to clean up and move to the Story Time Area.
- Thank the children for their kindness in helping to clean up.

Teach

Introduce the story.

- Ask the children, "Who knows what special day we will celebrate this week?" *(Valentine's Day)* Tell the children that Valentine's Day is named after Saint Valentine, a saint who showed his love for God and for people. Valentine's Day is a special day when we tell one another we love them.
- Show the children the teaching poster or the cover of the children's leaflet. Point to Carlos and invite the children to listen to what Carlos would do on Valentine's Day.

Tell the story.

Tell the children the name of the story "A Valentine's Day Hug." Refer to the teaching poster or the cover of the children's leaflet as you read the story to the children.

Recall the story.

- Help the children recall the key details of the story. Explain to them that you will need their help to remember the story. Read each of the following statements. When you come to the missing word ask: "Who can help me? Who can tell me the missing word?"

- Read each of the incomplete statements aloud. Provide clues as necessary to help the children recall the story:
  —Carlos was cutting out a big red ____. *(heart)*
  —Carlos was making the heart because tomorrow was ____. *(Valentine's Day)*
  —Carlos gave his father a big ____. *(hug)*
- Summarize by telling the children, "On Valentine's Day we do things to show our parents and friends that we love them."

Apply

Work on the children's leaflet activity.

- Ask several children to help you hand out the children's leaflet for this chapter. Have all the children look at the cover of the leaflet to help them recall the story.
- Ask the children to open their leaflet. Call their attention to the title "Show Love to Others," read it aloud and then explain the activity to the children. Invite the children to take turns telling about what they see in the pictures. Next, tell them to color the hearts next to the pictures of people showing someone that they love that person.
- Tell the children, "Jesus told us to love one another as he loves us. When we help people and are kind to people, we show them we love them. We are doing what Jesus told us to do."

Connect with the child's life.

- Ask the children to name one way they will show their love for their family this week. Congratulate them on their responses with brief responses, such as, "Giving your mom a hug is a wonderful way to show her you love her."
- Remind the children to take their leaflet home and to share the story on the For My Family Page and the activity with their family.
- Give them their heart pictures they made at the beginning of class. Encourage them to give their pictures to someone at home.

Show Love to Others

Find the pictures of people showing love. Color the hearts next to those pictures.

 Pray

- Gather the children at the prayer table. Invite the children to echo the words of the prayer "Thank you, God, for your love" after you.
- Call the children to a moment of silence. *(Pause.)* Lead the children in prayer. Begin with the Sign of the Cross.

Teacher: God our Father, you love us very much. Thank you, God, for your love.

Children: *Echo the words* "Thank you, God, . . ."

Teacher: God our Father, because you love us you give us people who love us and care for us. Thank you, God, for your love.

Children: *Echo the words* "Thank you, God, . . ."

Teacher: God our Father, help us show you how much we love you and help us show the people who love and care for us how much we love them. Together let us pray, "Amen."

All: Amen.

Additional Activities

Make and share heart shapes.
Use this activity to help the children show their love for someone by creating an "I Love You" heart.
- Tell the children that they are going to decorate two hearts, one to keep and one to share with another.
- Provide a variety of materials for the children to use to decorate their hearts, such as markers, paints, stickers, paper doilies and so on.
- Offer to write "I love you" on one of the two hearts for each of the children, and encourage them to give this heart to a friend or family member.

Share a Valentine Day snack.
Use this activity to create a Valentine's Day snack.
- Provide some bread, heart-shaped cookie cutters, plastic knives and some jelly or jam to spread over the bread.
- Help the children cut out heart shapes from pieces of bread, and use jelly or jam to decorate their heart-shaped pieces of bread.
- Remember to have the children wash their hands well before and after they make their heart sandwiches.
- Provide some cups for water or juice. Sit down together and have a sweet heart snack together.

CHAPTER 28 · We Love God More and More

Background
for the Catechist

Growing in Faith, Hope and Love

Lent is a time of celebration and hope! The days of Lent prepare us to celebrate Easter and welcome new members into the Church. The rites and observances of Lent invite us to grow in faith, hope and love, and to strengthen our union with Christ and our Church family.

Lent is a time of deepening our conversion to Christ. We examine our faith journey. We thank God for his grace that has enabled us to live as faithful disciples of Christ. We ask for his forgiveness for turning away from his love and for his grace to accept the gift of his love more faithfully.

During Lent, Christians focus on the disciplines of fasting, almsgiving and prayer. We pray for others and for ourselves. We sacrifice and give something up. We share our time and ourselves more generously with others, especially those in need. These traditional Lenten disciplines remind us that denial and struggle—taking up the cross each day—are essential dimensions of the life of a disciple of Jesus Christ.

For Reflection

How am I preparing my heart for the celebration of Easter? What can I do to guide my children to see Lent as a special time of the year to grow in their friendship with Jesus?

More Background

For further reading and reflection see *Catechism of the Catholic Church* §§ 540, 1095, 1430–1439, 1969; *Compendium—Catechism of the Catholic Church* §§ 106, 300–302; *United States Catholic Catechism for Adults* pages 173, 192–193, 238, 334, 518.

About the Children

Young children are known to tell tales that are, more often than not, based on fantasy. Young children do not clearly discriminate between fact and fiction very well. Their imaginations are more at work than their power of reason. When the children embellish the truth, they may appear to adults to be lying. However, their "tales" are not intentional lies as adults understand them. When young children share a tale with you or say something that is obviously not true, avoid jumping to the conclusion that the child is intentionally choosing to tell a lie.

A Few Suggestions . . .

Remember that telling tales is a normal developmental stage for all children. During this season of Lent, help the children grow in their ability to distinguish between fantasy and fact. Help them learn the difference between telling the truth and making things up or blaming others to get out of trouble. Simple statements, such as, "Anthony, that cannot be true," and an explanation of why their statement cannot be true will help the children begin to understand the importance of speaking truthfully. In all this, it is also important to encourage the children to correctly use their imaginations as they discover the goodness and beauty of the world, which is a manifestation of God's love.

Lesson Planner

Faith Focus

Every day we grow in our love for God and for others.

Story

"Kim Is Growing Up"

Materials Needed

In addition to the general supplies named on page 9 of this guide, you will need the following materials for teaching this lesson:

- small paper cups, one for each child; potting soil; scoop; fast-growing flower seeds, such as marigolds; spray bottle of water; foil
- baby picture
- punch-out figures of Kim

Enriching the Lesson

- RCL Benziger *Stories of God's Love* Music CD and companion Songbook, Song 1
- Visit our preschool Web site www.RCLBenzigerPreschool.com this week.

Prayer

God of compassion,
you invite us to deepen our love
for you and for others.
May we respond to your invitation.
Amen.

Chapter Objectives

After this week's lesson the children should be able to:

- recall the story "Kim Is Growing Up."
- discover that a part of growing up is learning to help others as God wants them to.
- demonstrate ways they are growing by helping others as friends of Jesus.

Kim Is Growing Up

28 We Love God More and More

Stories of God's Love Ages 3 and 4

Kim, Baby Mya and Grandma were sitting on the floor, playing with the blocks. Kim liked to stack the blocks and knock them over. Baby Mya would squeal and giggle every time.

Grandma said, "You have grown up so much, Kim."

"Was I ever as little as Mya?" Kim asked.

"Yes, you were as small as Baby Mya," Grandma answered.

"You mean I couldn't even stack the blocks?" asked Kim.

"My goodness, Honey, you were so little then that you could not even stack these blocks. You have learned to do so many things. You are growing up so much!" Grandma smiled and hugged Kim.

"I can do a lot of things," said Kim. "I can feed myself. I can color. I can run real fast. I even get to go to school to learn about God."

"That's right," said Grandma. "You have learned a lot. You are growing up at home, at school and at church. Every year you learn more ways you are part of our family here at home. Every year you will learn more ways to be part of our church family too."

"OK, Grandma, since I'm a big girl, can I have two scoops of ice cream when we finish playing blocks?" Kim asked.

Grandma smiled and gave her a big hug. "I think two scoops would be just right."

 ## Welcome

- Provide a packet of flower seeds (marigolds are a good choice, hardy and fast-growing), potting soil, a small scoop and small paper cups, one for each of the children.
- Greet the children by name and direct them to the Welcome Center. Show them the packet of seeds and other materials and ask, "Who can guess what we are going to do?" *(Plant seeds.)* Congratulate them for being so smart and guessing correctly. Open the seed packet and show the children the seeds. Tell them that these small seeds can grow up to be like the flower they see on the front. Then say, "We are going to plant seeds, but we are also going to take care of them and watch them grow."
- Hand out the paper cups and assist the children in scooping some potting soil and filling their cup three-quarters full. Demonstrate how they can plant the seeds by using their pointer finger to poke a shallow hole, put seeds in the soil and then lightly cover the seeds. Use a spray bottle to mist the soil. Note: If the children are going to take the planted seeds home, cover the cups with foil and secure the foil with rubber bands. Make sure to send a note home to parents explaining the activity.
- Work with the children to plant and water their seeds. Walk among them and talk about how each of them has grown and is learning to do more and more things on their own. Help the children understand that they are not only getting bigger and learning new things in school, they are growing more and more in their love for God.

 ## Gather

- Play the gathering song to signal that it is time for the children to clean up and move to the Story Time Area. Help the children wash their hands before going to the Story Time Area.
- Tell the children, "Our Church family celebrates this time of the year as a time of growing and this time has a special name. The name is *Lent*." Ask the children to echo the word *Lent* after you. Tell them, "Lent is a time of the year we do special things to show we love God more and more."
- Lead the children in singing this song to the tune of "It's Raining. It's Pouring":

    I'm growing. / You're growing. / Our love for God is showing. / In Lent we learn to love him more. / Our love for God is growing.

 ## Teach

Introduce the story.

- Show the children a picture of a baby. (If possible, show the children a picture of yourself when you were an infant.) Ask the children to tell you some things that they can do that a baby cannot do. Summarize by telling the children that all the things they named show that they are growing up.

- Call the children's attention to the teaching poster or show them the cover of the children's leaflet. Invite the children to listen as you tell a story about Kim and discover ways that she is growing up.

Tell the story.

Tell the children the name of the story "Kim Is Growing Up." Refer to the teaching poster or to the cover of the children's leaflet as you read the story to the children.

Recall the story.

- Help the children recall the details of the story. Explain to them that you will need their help to remember the story. Hand out the punch-out figures of Kim to the children. Tell them that you will name things in the story that show Kim was growing up. Ask them to raise the punch-out figure of Kim if what you tell them about Kim is true.
    —Kim was playing with her blocks. *(True)*
    —Kim said she can color. *(True)*
    —Kim said that she can feed herself. *(True)*
    —Kim said that she can cross the street by herself. *(Not True.)*
    —Kim said that she goes to school to learn about God. *(True)*
- Summarize by telling the children some of the ways you see that they are growing up. Be sure to include ways that they share things and work together. Praise the children for their achievements.

Apply

Work on the children's leaflet.

- Ask several children to help you hand out the children's leaflet for this chapter. Have all the children look at the cover to help them recall the story.
- Ask the children to open their leaflet and call their attention to the title "God Helps Me Grow in Love" and read it aloud to them. Explain to the children that Jesus told us that when we are kind to people and help them, we show that we love God too.
- Ask the children to look at the illustrations. Then have them look at the pictures, one at a time, and share what

they see happening in each of the pictures. Ask: "What do you see happening in this picture?" "How are the children being kind to one another?" Have them draw a happy face in the circle next to the pictures of children being kind to one another. Have them draw a sad face in the circle next to the picture of the child not being kind. Ask, "What can the child do to be kind to his friend?"

- Summarize by saying, "God wants us to grow big and strong. He wants us to grow in our love for him more and more each day. He wants us to show we love him by being kind to people."

Connect with the child's life.

- Tell the children we show that we love God when we are kind to people. Ask:
    —What is one way you can be kind at home?
    —What is one way you can be kind at school?
    —What is one way you can be kind when you play with your friends?
- Remind the children to take their leaflet home and to share the story and the activity with their family.

Pray

- Gather the children at the prayer table. Remind the children that when we pray we tell God we love him. Explain that they will echo the words of the prayer after you.
- Call the children to a moment of silence. *(Pause.)* Lead them in prayer. Begin with the Sign of the Cross.
    Dear God, *(Children echo the words.)* / you know I love you very much. *(Children echo the words.)* / Help me to love you more and more. *(Children echo the words.)* / Thank you. Amen. *(Children echo the words.)*
- Conclude by singing the song you sang with the children when they gathered in the Story Time Area.

Additional Activity
Make a Lent poster.
Use this activity to create a poster that you can use to hang in your learning area during Lent to remind the children of this special time of the year.

- Provide pictures of children of different ages and ethnic backgrounds cut out from magazines (or use pictures of the children that their parents have provided or you have taken in class during the year), a large poster with the heading "Lent: A Time to Grow in God's Love" and the words to the song you sang with the children during the Gathering time.
- Show the children the poster. Have them select and glue the pictures around the words of the song.
- Have the children gather near the poster throughout Lent and lead them in singing the song.

145

CHAPTER 29

We Celebrate Easter

Background
for the Catechist

The Lord Is Risen! Alleluia!
He Is Risen Indeed! Alleluia!

Christians are an Easter people! Alleluia is our song. The word *Alleluia* means "Praise the Lord God." We praise God for raising Jesus from the dead to new life. On the third day after his death on the cross and his burial in the tomb Jesus was raised from the dead.

The mystery of Jesus' Resurrection lies at the heart of faith in Christ. It is both a real event and a true mystery of faith. It is the source of our hope in our own resurrection and eternal life in communion with God the Father, God the Son and God the Holy Spirit. The Resurrection of Christ so became the focus of Sunday for Christians that every Sunday became a "little Easter."

At Easter we see signs of new life in nature all around us that the children are familiar with. There are tulips, daffodils, lilies, butterflies, baby chicks, growing grass and leaves appearing on trees. All these signs remind Christians of the Resurrection. They remind us that joined to Christ in Baptism we too will journey through death to new life as he did. Alleluia!

For Reflection

In what ways is the Resurrection of Christ the cornerstone of my faith? What can I do to show the children that Jesus is always present with us?

More Background

For further reading and reflection see *Catechism of the Catholic Church* §§ 638–655; 1166–1171; *Compendium—Catechism of the Catholic Church* §§ 125–131, 241; *United States Catholic Catechism for Adults* pages 93-96, 510, 525.

About the Children

Young children have a natural sense of wonder and awe that intuitively places them in the presence of God and in communion with him. Parents and teachers need to be aware of this quality that is so characteristic of young people. What might seem to be simple child's play to an adult, for example, staring at or playing with an earthworm or smelling a flower, can be a moment of exploration. Such experiences can put a child in touch with the unseen presence of God in their lives. Adults need to appreciate this sense of wonder and awe at work in the life of children.

A Few Suggestions . . .

Parents and teachers need to develop skills that enable them to be silent observers and listeners. Take advantage of your outdoor space. Observe the children as they explore the world around them and really listen to the questions they have and the comments they make. For example, if you see a child watching a bug crawling along, stop, observe and listen. Resist interrupting their attention by asking questions, such as, "What do you see on the bottom of the worm?" Join them in their explorations, in their wonder and awe. Your presence will invite the conversation. Enter their world and connect the lessons to the experiences.

Lesson Planner

Faith Focus

Jesus is alive. He is always with us.

Story

"Grandpa Keeps His Promises"

Enriching the Lesson

- RCL Benziger *Stories of God's Love* Music CD and companion Songbook, Song 1
- Visit our preschool Web site www.RCLBenzigerPreschool.com this week.

Chapter Objectives

After this week's lesson the children should be able to:

- recall the story "Grandpa Keeps His Promises."
- discover that Jesus is alive. He is always with us.
- celebrate being friends of Jesus who is always with us.

Materials Needed

In addition to the general supplies named on page 9 of this guide, you will need the following materials for teaching this lesson:

- sheets of dark-colored construction paper, one for each child
- green construction paper cut into shapes of leaves and stems and
- pastel construction paper cut into flower petals, enough for each child to make a flower
- punch-out figures of Jamal

Prayer

Lord Jesus,
you have risen indeed.
Alleluia!
We live in your presence.
Let us rejoice always.
Alleluia!
Amen.

Grandpa Keeps His Promises

It was Easter Sunday and Jamal and his family were getting ready to visit with Grandpa. "I love to visit Grandpa in the big city," said Jamal. "We are going to play today, just Grandpa and me!"

"How do you know?" asked Mom.

"He promised me and we always play together," said Jamal.

As soon as they arrived at Grandpa's home, Jamal knocked on the door. Grandpa answered the door and gave Jamal, his mom and his dad a big hug. Before anyone could say anything else, Jamal asked, "Grandpa, do you remember your promise?"

Smiling at Jamal, Grandpa said, "Of course I remember! Come on in and let's play."

"Yeah!" shouted Jamal as he jumped up and down. "I told you Grandpa would remember."

As he was playing with Jamal Grandpa asked, "Jamal, do you remember what special day it is today?"

Jamal looked a little confused so Grandpa said, "Today is Easter Sunday. Today we are all going to church together. On Easter we celebrate that Jesus is alive. He kept his special promise to always be with us."

"So, let's play our board game, and then it's off to church we go," Grandpa said.

Later on as Jamal rode back home with his parents from Grandpa's home in the big city, Jamal said, "I love Grandpa so much."

Dad said, "And Grandpa loves you too. That's why he always keeps his promises to you."

"Right, Daddy. I'm going to be just like Grandpa when I grow up!"

 Welcome

- Provide glue, sheets of dark-colored construction paper, leaf-shapes and stem-shapes cut out from green construction paper and flower petals cut out from pastel-colored paper, enough materials for each of the children to make a flower.
- Greet the children by name and direct them to the Welcome Center. Remind them that it is springtime. Ask: "What new things do you see in the spring?" "What new sounds do you hear in the spring?" Add things the children did not name. Summarize by saying, "In the spring we see many things coming alive."
- Show the children the flower that you made in preparation for teaching today's lesson. Note: If you did the seed planting activity during Lent, show them your new flower.
- Call their attention to the materials and explain the activity. Help the children glue the stem, leaves and petals on construction paper to make their flowers. Write or help the children write their names on their completed pictures.
- Assist the children in placing their pictures somewhere to dry.

 Gather

- Play the gathering song to signal that it is time for the children to clean up and move to the Story Time Area.
- Tell the children, "In the springtime of each year our church family celebrates the most important time of the year for the friends of Jesus. That time of the year is named *Easter*." Say the word *Easter* aloud and have the children echo it after you. Explain that during Easter we celebrate a special promise Jesus made to us. Jesus is alive. He is always with us.

 Teach

Introduce the story.

- Tell the children,
  —"Raise your hands if you have ever heard the word *promise*?" (*Invite children to raise their hands.*)
  —"Now raise your hands if you can tell me what it means to make a promise." (*Invite and listen to responses.*)
- Conclude by telling the children, "To make a promise is to tell someone that you will do something good and that you will do what you tell them."
- Call the children's attention to the teaching poster or show them the cover of the children's leaflet. Tell them that today's lesson is about Easter. Have them echo the word *Easter* after you and remind them what you told them about Easter in the Welcome Center. (*During Easter we celebrate a special promise Jesus made to us and that he kept. Jesus is alive and he is always with us.*)
- Have the children look at the teaching poster or the cover of the children's leaflet once again. Invite them to listen to

a story about Jamal and discover the special promises Grandpa made to him and how he kept his promises.

Tell the story.

Tell the children the name of the story "Grandpa Keeps His Promises." Refer to the teaching poster or the cover of the children's leaflet as you read the story to the children.

Recall the story.

- Help the children recall the key details of the story. Explain to them that you will need their help to remember the story. Ask, "Who would like to help me remember the story we just listened to?" *(Pause.)*
- Hand out the punch-out figures of Jamal to each of the children. Tell them, "I will ask you some questions about the story. I will stop after each question and ask you to hold up your figure of Jamal if you know the answer to the question. Then I will ask everyone who is holding up their figure of Jamal to tell me the answer to the question together. Let's begin."
    - —Who was Jamal going to visit? *(Grandpa)*
    - —What did Grandpa make to Jamal? *(A promise)*
    - —Did Grandpa keep his promise? *(Yes)*
    - —On what special day did Jamal visit his Grandpa? *(Easter)*
    - —Where did Grandpa take Jamal and his family on Easter? *(To church)*
- Thank the children for helping you remember the story and congratulate them for remembering it so well.

Apply

Work on the children's leaflet activity.

- Ask several children to help you hand out the children's leaflet for this chapter. Have all the children look at the cover to help them recall the story.
- Ask the children to open their leaflet. Call their attention to the title and read it aloud to them. Have them look at the pictures, one at a time, connect the dots and tell you what the pictures remind them about Easter. Provide the children with clues, if necessary, to help them talk about the pictures. For example, explain that the lily looks like a

trumpet. The sound of a trumpet fills the air with the sounds of great joy. On Easter we are filled with joy because Jesus is alive and always with us. If time permits, have them color the pictures.

- Summarize by saying, "Easter is the most important time of the year for the friends of Jesus. We are filled with joy. Jesus kept his promise. He is alive and always with us."

Connect with the child's life.

- Ask the children, "What is one thing you can tell your family about Easter?" Listen to their responses, clarify as needed and encourage them to tell their families about Easter.
- Remind the children to take their leaflet home and to share the story and the activity with their family.

Pray

- Display in the Prayer Area the flower pictures the children made at the beginning of class. (Optional: Also decorate the prayer table with brightly colored flowers.)
- Gather the children at the prayer table. Explain to the children that they will pray a special prayer word today as their part of the prayer. Tell them the word is *Alleluia*. Say the word *Alleluia* again and have the children echo it after you.
- Call the children to a moment of silence. *(Pause.)* Lead the children in prayer. Begin with the Sign of the Cross.

  Teacher: Jesus is alive.
  Alleluia! Alleluia! Alleluia!
  Children: Alleluia! Alleluia! Alleluia!
  Teacher: Jesus is always with us.
  Alleluia! Alleluia! Alleluia!
  Children: Alleluia! Alleluia! Alleluia!

- Conclude by playing a lively recording of the singing of "Alleluia" and invite the children to follow you and process around the room to the music and join you in singing "Alleluia."

Additional Activity

Make mosaic Easter crosses.

Use this activity to create a traditional symbol of Easter to remind the children that Jesus is always with us.

- Provide cross shapes made from white construction paper, small pieces of paper cut from a variety of brightly colored constructions paper, glitter and glue, enough materials for each of the children.
- Show the children the mosaic Easter cross that you made in preparation for this lesson and explain how you made it. Hand out a construction paper cross shape to each of the children. Show them the other materials and work with them to make their Easter crosses.

It Is Easter

Connect the dots.
Discover and color the Easter pictures.

We Love Mary

Background
for the Catechist

We Honor Mary

The Church around the world honors Mary, the Mother of Jesus, the Mother of the Church. We remember Mary's faith, her hope, her love for God and her loving faithfulness to her Son.

Since the earliest days of the Church, Christians have looked upon Mary as our Mother, the Mother of all Christians. We believe and trust that Mary cares for us, watches over us and wants us to grow closer to her Son, Jesus.

Catholics honor Mary and express their devotion to her throughout the year. At Mass we recognize Mary's presence with us and honor her. Mary joins with us and her Son in giving God the Father praise and thanksgiving through the power of the Holy Spirit.

During Advent we remember Mary as the one who brings Jesus into the world. During Lent and Holy Week, we remember Mary, the Mother of Sorrows. During Easter we look forward to joining Mary and the saints in Heaven.

For Reflection

What do I do to show my love and honor for Mary? What symbols have I placed or can I place within the classroom to remind the children of Mary's love for them?

About the Children

As children get closer to kindergarten age, they take a cognitive leap that often baffles the adults who live and work with them. For example, you will notice that their use of language becomes more complex. It is important for both parents and teachers to support the children during this stage of their growth. Responding patiently and positively to the children as they use their new skills to try new things will contribute to their growth in confidence and growing independence and will encourage their desire to learn.

A Few Suggestions . . .

As you accompany the children through their learning and growth, it is important to show them that you respect them and their efforts at learning new things. Respecting the children includes giving them your genuine attention, listening to their concerns and responding to them with reassurance and sensitivity. Seeing you model these behaviors is the best way for pre-kindergarteners to learn to show others respect.

More Background

For further reading and reflection see *Catechism of the Catholic Church* §§ 963–972, *Compendium—Catechism of the Catholic Church* §§ 196–199, *United States Catholic Catechism for Adults* pages 141–149.

Lesson Planner

Faith Focus

We love Mary. We show Mary we love her.

Story

"Mary Loves Us"

Materials Needed

In addition to the general supplies named on page 9 of this guide, you will need the following materials for teaching this lesson:

- pieces of white paper with the name *Mary* written on them in white crayon, one for each of the children
- watercolor paints, paint brushes and small cups of water, enough materials for all children to share
- punch-out figures of Abby

Enriching the Lesson

- RCL Benziger *Stories of God's Love* Music CD and companion Songbook, Song 1
- Visit our preschool Web site www.RCLBenzigerPreschool.com this week.

Chapter Objectives

After this week's lesson the children should be able to:

- recall the story "Mary Loves Us."
- discover that Mary loves them as a mother loves her children.
- show Mary their love.

Prayer

Mary, my Mother,
I turn to you, trusting in your love.
Teach me to love God
and my neighbor as myself
as your only Son, Jesus, commanded.
May the example of my words and actions
guide the children to grow
in their love for you.
Amen.

Mary Loves Us

Abby was rocking her baby doll to sleep. She looked over to her mother and said, "Mommy, I love my baby so much. I want to be a mommy just like you when I grow up."

Abby laid her baby on the blanket in her crib and said, "Shhh, Mommy. We have to be quiet now. My baby is sleeping."

Tiptoeing out of the room, Abby and her mommy went to the kitchen for a snack. Abby chose an apple. So did her mommy.

Abby said, "Mommy, at school Miss Diaz told us that the name of Jesus' Mother was Mary. Was she a mommy like you?" Abby asked.

Abby's mommy smiled and said, "Yes, Sweetie. Mary loved Jesus very, very much. She took care of Jesus when he was a baby. She helped him learn how to do things. She prayed with him. Mary was a very special mommy."

"You know, Abby," her mommy said, "Mary loves you and me and all the friends of Jesus in a special way too. She is with Jesus in Heaven. We can tell her how much we love her too."

Abby gave her mommy a hug and said, "I love you, Mommy. And I love Mary. Now let's go see if my baby is ready to get up from her nap."

 ## Welcome

- Provide sheets of white unlined paper on which you have printed the name *Mary* with a white crayon, one sheet of paper for each of the children. Also provide dark-colored, thinned-out watercolor paint, paintbrushes and small cups of water, enough materials for all the children to share.
- Greet the children by name and direct them to the Welcome Center. Tell them that today they will be learning more about a very special person whom they learned about at Christmas.
- Show the children the art materials and tell them that the name of that special person is hidden on the paper. Demonstrate how to dip the paintbrush into the paint and then into the cup of water and very lightly brush the paint on the paper to discover the name of the special person. *(Mary)*
- Walk among the children as they are working on the activity and help them as needed.
- Show the children the painting that you completed in preparation for teaching this lesson. Point to the name Mary and read it aloud to the children and have them echo it after you.
- Have them look at their paintings and say the name Mary aloud. Then ask, "Who would like to tell me who Mary is?" *(Mary is Jesus' mother.)* Congratulate the children for recognizing Mary's name and telling you who Mary is.
- Help the children write their names on their painting. Collect the paintings and put them in a place to dry. Note: The children will use their paintings during the closing prayer.

 ## Gather

- Play the gathering song to signal that it is time for the children to clean up and move to the Story Time Area.
- Take special care to encourage all of the children to help clean up today. Make sure the children conduct the clean-up by themselves today.

 ## Teach

Introduce the story.

- Show the children the teaching poster or the cover of the children's leaflet.
- Call the children's attention to the illustration of Abby and her mother and invite the children to listen to today's story and discover what Abby told her mommy about Mary.

Tell the story.

Tell the children the name of today's story "Mary Loves Us." Refer to the teaching poster or to the cover of the children's leaflet as you read the story to the children.

Recall the story.

- Help the children recall the key details of the story. Explain to them that you will need their help to remember the story. Ask, "Who would like to help me remember the story we just listened to?" *(Pause.)* Thank everyone.
- Hand out the punch-out figures of Abby to each of the children. Tell them, "I will pretend to be Abby's mommy and you all will pretend to be Abby. I will tell you some parts of the story. I will stop after each part I tell you and ask you to hold up your figure of Abby if what I tell you really happened in the story.
    —Abby told her mommy that her teacher told her that the name of Jesus' mother was Mary. *(Yes)*
    —Abby's mommy told her that Mary loved Jesus very, very much. *(Yes)*
    —Abby's mommy told her that Mary loves her and all the friends of Jesus in a special way. *(Yes)*
    —Abby told her mom, "I love Mary." *(Yes)*
- Conclude by telling the children that our Church family shows that we love Mary in many, many ways.

 Apply

Work on the children's leaflet activity.

- Ask several children to help you hand out the children's leaflet for this chapter. Have all the children look at the cover of the children's leaflet to help them recall the story. Remind the children that Abby and her mommy talked about how much Mary loves Jesus and that Mary loves them and all the friends of Jesus too.
- Ask the children to open their leaflet. Call their attention to the title "My Prayer to Mary" and read it aloud to them.
- Tell the children that in today's activity they will color and pray a prayer to Mary.
- Explain the directions for the activity and have the children work on it.
- Walk among the children as they are working on the activity. Remind them of Mary's love for them.
- Conclude by leading the children in praying the prayer. Pray it aloud and have the children pray it quietly in their hearts. Make sure they say their own name at the end of the prayer.

My Prayer to Mary

MARY,
God loves you.
I love you very much too.

Color the word. Write your name.
Pray your prayer to Mary.

Connect with the child's life.

- Ask the children, "When can you pray to Mary and tell her you love her?" Congratulate the children on their responses.
- Remind the children to take home their leaflet and share the story and activity with their family.

 Pray

- Cover the prayer table with a blue cloth, place a statue or picture of Mary on the prayer table and decorate the prayer table with flowers.
- Gather the children in the Story Time Area. Explain to them that today's prayer will be a special prayer to Mary. Hand out their paintings of the name *Mary*. Tell them that they will walk behind and carry their paintings of the name *Mary* to the Prayer Area. Explain that walking this way is a special way to pray. It is called *walking in procession*. Demonstrate the following prayer to Mary and tell the children that they will pray it with you at the prayer table:
    Holy Mary *(hands at waist, outstretched and moving forward)*, / we love you *(hands and arms folded at chest)*. / Mother of Jesus *(hands cradled as rocking a baby)*, / and our mother *(open hands and point to chest)* / we love you *(hands and arms folded at chest)*. Amen. *(hold hands together in prayer gesture)*
- Call the children to a moment of silence. *(Pause.)* Lead the children in procession to the prayer table. Gather around the prayer table with the children and lead them in prayer. Begin with the Sign of the Cross.

Additional Activity

Make prayer cards.

Use this activity to help the children remember to tell Mary how much they love her.

- Provide crayons and markers and 4-inch by 6-inch unlined index cards cut in half lengthwise on which you have written the prayer "Holy Mary, we love you," one card for each of the children.
- Hand out the cards to the children. Read the prayer on the card aloud to them. Have the children echo the prayer after you several times to help them learn the prayer by heart.
- Ask the children to trace the letters of the words of the prayer and decorate their prayer cards, using crayons or markers. Tell them to pray the prayer quietly in their hearts as they are decorating their prayer cards.
- Tell the children to take their finished prayer cards home and show the cards to their family. Ask them to place them near their bed and pray to Mary each morning when they wake up and each night before they go to sleep.

Chapter 3 • Activity Master   **Jesus Is the Good Shepherd**   *Stories of God's Love Ages 3 and 4*

Stories of God's Love Ages 3 and 4   The Good Shepherd Cares for His Sheep   **Chapter 5** • Activity Master

Chapter 10 • Activity Master   **I Take Care of Myself**   *Stories of God's Love Ages 3 and 4*

Stories of God's Love Ages 3 and 4   Jesus Is Born   **Chapter 11** • Activity Master

_____

name

I invite you to visit my religion class on

_____

date

_____

time

at

_____

location

_____

child's name

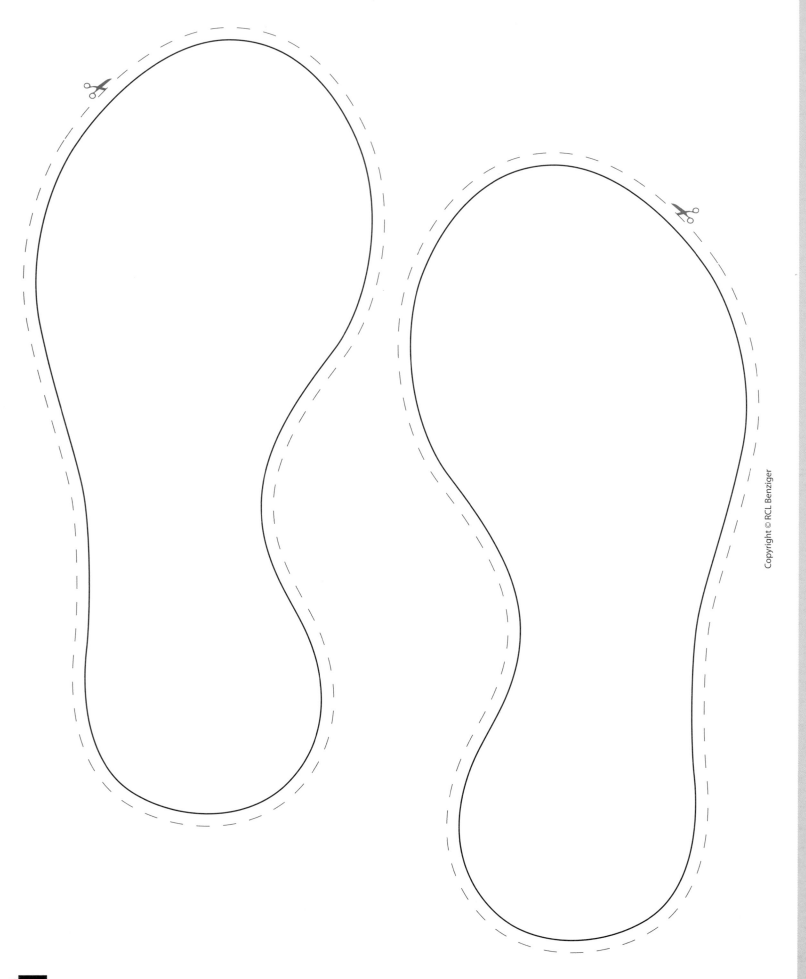

We Celebrate Christmas *Stories of God's Love Ages 3 and 4*

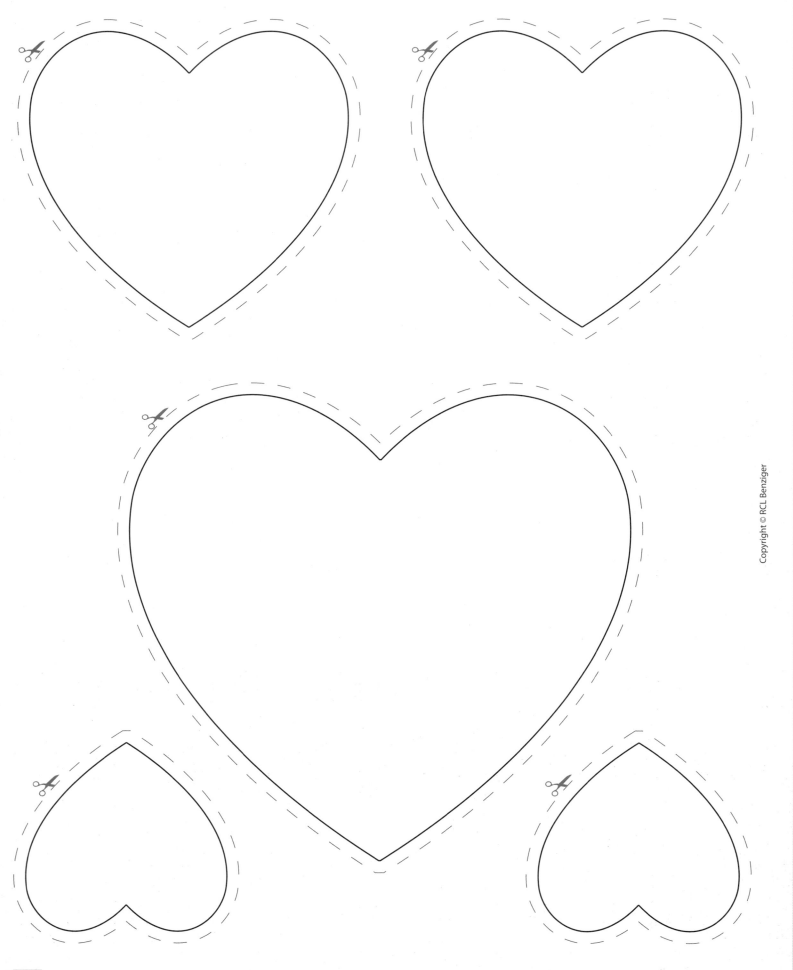

Chapter 27 • Activity Master 1 **Valentine's Day** *Stories of God's Love Ages 3 and 4*

Love One Another

Love One Another

Love One Another

Love One Another

Love One Another